PUBLISHED VOLUMES

1. *The Diary and Related Writings of the Reverend Joseph Dimock (1768-1846).* Ed. George E. Levy. 1979.

2. *Repent and Believe: The Baptist Experience in Maritime Canada.* Ed. Barry M. Moody. 1980.

3. *The Journal of the Reverend John Payzant (1749-1834).* Ed. Brian C. Cuthbertson. 1981.

4. *The Life and Journal of the Rev. Mr. Henry Alline.* Ed. James Beverley and Barry M. Moody. 1982.

5. *The New Light Letters and Spiritual Songs.* Ed. George Rawlyk. 1983.

6. *The Newlight Baptist Journals of James Manning and James Innis.* Ed. D.G. Bell. 1984.

7. *The Sermons of Henry Alline.* Ed. George A. Rawlyk. 1986.

THE SERMONS OF HENRY ALLINE

BAPTIST HERITAGE IN ATLANTIC CANADA

Documents and Studies

A Series Sponsored by

Acadia Divinity College
(Wolfville, Nova Scotia)

and

The Baptist Historical Committee ·
(United Baptist Convention of the Atlantic Provinces)

EDITORIAL COMMITTEE

Jarold K. Zeman, Chairman
(Acadia Divinity College, Wolfville, N.S.)

Phyllis R. Blakeley
(Public Archives of Nova Scotia, Halifax, N.S.)

Barry M. Moody
(Acadia University, Wolfville, N.S.)

George A. Rawlyk
(Queen's University, Kingston, Ontario)

Robert Wilson
(Atlantic Baptist College, Moncton, N.B.)

THE SERMONS
OF
HENRY ALLINE

edited by

George A. Rawlyk

Published by
LANCELOT PRESS
for
Acadia Divinity College and
The Baptist Historical Committee of the
United Baptist Convention of the Atlantic Provinces
1986

ISBN 0-88999-310-6

COPYRIGHT 1986 by Acadia Divinity College

Published and distributed by
Lancelot Press Limited,
P.O. Box 425,
Hantsport, N.S., Canada B0P 1P0

CONTENTS

For
Ron Noble and Mark Parent
whose sermons
have meant so much to me.

GENERAL EDITORS' PREFACE

The search for personal and family roots has become a popular pursuit in our days. It has also rekindled interest in the history of local churches and denominational bodies. A church without the knowledge of its history is like a man who has lost his memory. Historical amnesia is a dangerous disease which afflicts much of contemporary church life.

The purpose of the series BAPTIST HERITAGE IN ATLANTIC CANADA is to make available, over a period of years, a collection of primary sources and critical studies dealing with the historical development of the Baptist witness in the Atlantic provinces of Canada.

In the three Maritime provinces (Nova Scotia, New Brunswick and Prince Edward Island) Baptist congregations have existed for more than two centuries, and in several counties constitute the largest religious body today. By contrast, Baptist churches were introduced to Newfoundland only three decades ago. Through migration, family ties, exchange of leaders and other means of contact, Baptists of the Maritime provinces have exerted significant influence on the spiritual and cultural life in Central and Western Canada, as well as in the Eastern United States, particularly in New England. Most materials planned for publication in the series should, therefore, be of more than regional interest.

The Editorial Committee formulates general policy and guidelines for the series, and selects works to be published.

Editors or authors of particular volumes assume full responsibility for the content and quality of their work.

The publication of the series is sponsored by Acadia Divinity College and the Baptist Historical Committee of the United Baptist Convention of the Atlantic Provinces, in cooperation with Lancelot Press (William Pope).

Gifts for the project will be appreciated and will make it possible for the Editorial Committee to publish additional volumes without undue delays. Donations may be sent to Acadia Divinity College (Wolfville, N.S., B0P 1X0) and designated for "Baptist Heritage Publication Fund."

Jarold K. Zeman
Chairperson
Editorial Committee

ACKNOWLEDGEMENTS

I owe a great deal to Ms. Sharon Judd, Ms. Susan Young, and Mrs. Linda Freeman, who have typed parts of this manuscript. I am also indebted to Mr. David Bell and Professor Stephen Marini who have carefully read it and who have made a number of valuable suggestions as to how the introduction could be improved.

Most of the research for this volume has been funded by the Advisory Research Committee of the School of Graduate Studies and Research, Queen's University, and by the University Consortium for Research on North America, Harvard University. The publication of the book has been generously supported by subventions from the Jackman Foundation, Toronto, and from the School of Graduate Studies and Research, Queen's University. I am also very grateful for the tremendous support and encouragement given to me, over the years, by Professor J.K. Zeman of Acadia Divinity College. He has, among other things, helped me to redefine significantly my "research agenda."

A NOTE ON EDITING

In a particularly discerning review-article entitled "Clio and the Historical Editor,"* Professor J.M. Bumsted has laid down what he considers to be the "minimum to be expected from an editor." He stresses five essentials — "both from the standpoint of scholarship abstractly considered and from that of the book-purchasing public." These five essentials are:

> (1) an accurate text, and some explicit statement of the transcription style employed, (2) a complete text or some editorial explanation and justification of any omissions, (3) an editorial introduction which provides an adequate context for the printed transcription, especially for the non-specialist reader, (4) sufficient annotation to clarify obscure references in the text, including those to characters and situations given more than fleeting mention by the original author, and (5) a full index.

What follows is my attempt to deal with the five points raised by Professor Bumsted. I have tried to provide an accurate and complete text within a detailed historical context, and I have

---

* J.M. Bumsted, "Clio and the Historical Editor," *Acadiensis*, Vol. IX, No. 2 (Spring, 1980), p. 92.

also been concerned about adding suitable and sufficient annotations as well as a "full index."

As far as the transcription is concerned, I have attempted to copy accurately the original texts of the printed sermons and also the Reverend Jonathan Scott's printed assessment of one of Alline's sermons. I have not modernized any of the spellings and I have only added in square brackets the missing letters or words necessary to understand their actual meaning. As far as punctuation is concerned, I have endeavoured to replicate the original, however inconsistent it might be. Alline's writing was characterized by its "stream of consciousness" quality and he certainly had little grasp of the meaning of a comma, a period or a semi-colon. His words flowed relentlessly on — in a myriad of directions — as the Spirit moved him.

Copies of Alline's two Liverpool printed sermons (1782) are to be found in the Acadia University Archives, Wolfville, Nova Scotia; *A Sermon Preached on the 19th of February at Fort-Midway* is deposited in the John Carter Brown Library, Providence, Rhode Island. Scott's *Brief View* is available in the Congregational Library, Boston, Massachusetts.

INTRODUCTION

Since 1972, it may be effectively argued, no Maritimer has received as much scholarly attention from the historical community as has Henry Alline. The growing interest in the charismatic Nova Scotia preacher has been such that it has been recently noted "that we may yet see Henry Alline supplant Joseph Howe as the world's favourite Nova Scotian."[1] According to David Bell, moreover, the resulting transformation of Maritime religious historiography has been "little short of miraculous."[2] And as a direct consequence, post-Revolutionary Maritime religious history, with its emphasis on the Allinite legacy, has now formed what is to some the cutting edge of the discipline in Canada. The caustic critic might comment that, taking into account the sad state of contemporary Canadian religious historiography, such a claim is indeed a modest one. Nevertheless, even those scholars who have and have had serious reservations about the historical importance of Alline cannot, in all conscience, close their eyes both to the quality and quantity of material recently written about the "Whitefield of Nova Scotia."[3]

I

Henry Alline was born in Newport, Rhode Island, in 1748 and in 1760 he moved with his parents and hundreds of other Yankees to the Minas Basin region of Nova Scotia. The

7

Alline family settled in Falmouth where the young Alline worked on his father's farm and then, in his twenties, developed certain skills in tanning and currying. There was little in Alline's Nova Scotia upbringing to suggest that he would develop into one of the region's great preachers and hymn writers.[4]

At the age of twenty-seven, in the early months of 1775, Alline experienced a profound spiritual crisis, and then an exhilarating conversion. He felt compelled soon afterwards to share his new-found faith and salvation first with his neighbours, then with other Nova Scotians, and then, just when he was on the verge of death, with republican New England. The charismatic Alline helped trigger Nova Scotia's so-called First Great Awakening — a widespread and intense religious revival which swept through much of what is now Nova Scotia and New Brunswick during the middle and latter part of the American Revolution. The Awakening was one of the significant social movements in the long history of Nova Scotia. Alline's preaching provided the means whereby many disoriented and confused Nova Scotians, especially recently arrived Yankees like himself, were able to find some real meaning in the "Confusion, Trouble and Anguish"[5] which had descended on the colony because of the often frenzied tensions unleashed by the American Revolution.

Alline's preaching was permeated by a preoccupation with disintegrating, disintegrated and renewed relationships. Generalizing from his own traumatic religious experience — the ravishing ecstasy of his own regeneration — Alline emphasized that every Nova Scotian could emulate him if only they reached out, in faith, to Christ. In a world where all traditional relationships were falling apart, a personal "interest in Christ," as Alline put it, created by the "New Birth," was the means whereby all these threatened relationships would be strengthened. Conversion was, therefore, perceived by Alline and his followers as "the short-circuiting of a complex process — a short-circuiting which produced instant and immediate satisfaction, solace, and intense relief."[6] The Awakening was, in one sense, a collection of these positive individual experiences and helped to give shape and substance to a new and distinct Nova Scotia sense of identity. And it was Alline's powerfully charismatic and evangelical preaching and not his published work which significantly shaped the contours of the First Great Awakening.[7]

During the 1778 to 1783 period, Alline visited almost every settlement in Nova Scotia, then inhabited by approximately 20,000 persons. The area included present-day New Brunswick. Halifax, Lunenburg and Pictou, all non-Yankee settlements, were the only major centres of the colony unaffected by the religious "reformation" in which he played a key role. Almost single-handedly, as he criss-crossed the colony, Alline was able to draw many of the isolated communities together and to give them a fragile feeling of oneness. The hundreds of people involved, whether core or peripheral participants, were all sharing a common experience — a religious awakening — and Alline was providing them with spiritual answers to disconcerting and puzzling contemporary questions. For Alline — and this must have also been the case for many of his followers — the Nova Scotia revival was, at its core, an event of world, even cosmic significance. While New England and Old England were involved in what Alline regarded as an evil civil war, Nova Scotia was experiencing a remarkable work of God. As far as Alline was concerned, the revival provided convincing proof that the Nova Scotians were — as he once expressed it — "a people on whom God has set His everlasting Love" and that their colony was "as the Apple of His Eye."[8]

The implication of the conjunction of events, of civil war in neighbouring New England and an unprecedented outpouring of the Holy Spirit in Nova Scotia, must have been obvious to Alline and to the thousands who flocked to hear him. The Almighty, the evidence more than suggested, was transferring New England's special mantle of Evangelical Christian leadership to Nova Scotia — "New England's Outpost."[9] With Republican and Revolutionary New England rushing madly off course, it could no longer provide the solid Evangelical base from which positive Christianity could spread its enlightened influence throughout the world in preparation for the return of Christ. Moreover, as has been argued elsewhere,

With two powerful Protestant nations furiously battling one another, the whole course of events since the Reformation seemed to be ending in a meaningless tangle. In the world view of those New Englanders fighting for the Revolutionary cause, Old England was corrupt and the Americans were engaged in a righteous and noble cause. There was therefore some meaning for hostilities.[10]

But for Alline and his followers, the Revolutionary War had no such meaning. Rather, in conjunction with the Nova Scotia Revival, the war could indicate only one thing. Alline's Nova Scotia — a largely backward frontier settlement of no consequence — had in fact been suddenly transformed by "the remarkable providences of God"[11] into *the* "Redeemer Nation."[12]

II

It was Alline's charismatic preaching that gave shape and substance to Nova Scotia's First Great Awakening. His two contemporary published books did not. The *Two Mites on Some of the Most Important and much disputed Points of Divinity* (Halifax, 1781) and *The Anti-Traditionist* (Halifax, 1783) were not widely read in the colony. If anything, his *Two Mites* — a convoluted anti-Calvinist work, permeated by what Maurice Armstrong once referred to as "Alline's peculiar doctrines"[13] — probably helped to dampen the revival fire. These two books tell us a great deal about Alline's theology which, according to one contemporary, was a strange mixture of "Calvinism, Antinomianism and Enthusiasm."[14] But the *Two Mites* and *The Anti-Traditionist* — both full of "rhetorical and extravagant"[15] views — shed little real light on the Awakening, and on Alline's charismatic powers. Alline's *Journal*, however, does. Yet the *Journal* was not published until 1806 even though a manuscript version of the published document was in circulation, among Alline's followers, soon after his death in February, 1784.[16] The *Journal* provides a superb introspective and illuminating account of the spiritual travails of an unusually gifted eighteenth-century North American mystic and preacher.

During his lifetime, Alline also published a tiny volume of twenty-two hymns, *Hymns and Spiritual Songs On a Variety of Pleasing and Important Subjects.* Then two years after his death, his *Hymns and Spiritual Songs* which contained 488 original hymns and spiritual songs, was printed in Boston.[17] Eventually, at least four editions of this volume were published in the United States. The extraordinary popularity of Alline's *Hymns and Spiritual Songs* in both the United States and in New Brunswick and Nova Scotia provide convincing proof that Alline had succeeded in making his hymns and spiritual songs communicate deep religious truths to ordinary believers. Alline used simple "sensuous imagery, subjectivism, and Biblical paraphrase"[18] in order to articulate religious concepts which largely uneducated people could understand and could resonate with. His hymns and songs, in other words, "represented the common denominator of plain-folk religious belief."[19]

Because of its pivotal importance in understanding both Alline and Nova Scotia's First Great Awakening, it is not surprising that the complete text of the *Journal* was reprinted in 1982 in this series, and that almost one-third of the *Journal* appeared in the same year, in Gordon Stewart's Champlain Society edition of *Documents Relating to the Great Awakening in Nova Scotia, 1760-1791.*[20] Moreover, many of Alline's most popular hymns and spiritual songs were reprinted in my *New Light Letters and Songs,* published in 1983. A year earlier Thomas Vincent had made available a few of Alline's compositions in his *Selected Hymns and Spiritual Songs of Henry Alline.*[21]

Yet despite the fact that Gordon Stewart has convincingly argued that Alline's sermons and his preaching are of central and crucial importance in understanding the man and the religious movement he helped to create, there has been, since the last decade of the 18th century, little apparent interest in Alline's sermon literature. Professor Stewart is, of course, a noteable exception since the core of his thesis concerning the symbiotic relationship between Alline and his Nova Scotia listeners is dependent on Alline's preaching message, and how it was perceived by his contemporaries.[22]

It is noteworthy that before Stewart's thesis was completed in 1971 those authors who wrote about Alline either did not even consult his sermons, or else significantly underplayed their importance. For example, W. B. Bezanson, *The Romance of Religion: A Sketch of the Life of Henry Alline* (Kentville, 1927) did not make use of any of the sermons, nor did E. W. Eldridge who in 1948 wrote a B.D. thesis on "Henry Alline: The Apostle of Nova Scotia" at Andover-Newton Theological School. That same year, two influential Canadian scholars — one teaching in Canada and the other in the United States — wrote important books dealing with, among other things, Henry Alline. In his seminal *Church and Sect in Canada*,[23] the sociologist S. D. Clark saw Alline largely through the prism of his *Journal* and did not make use of any of Alline's sermons in his suggestive chapter entitled "The Great Awakening in Nova Scotia." In *The Great Awakening in Nova Scotia* Maurice Armstrong also placed great stress on Alline's *Journal* but underscored also the importance of *Two Mites, The Anti-Traditionist* and *Hymns and Spiritual Songs.* Concerning Alline's three sermons, Armstrong was content to write only four paragraphs. According to Armstrong:

> Although he preached many times a week, it was always extemporaneously; accordingly, Henry Alline's sermons are for the most part forever lost. Three sermons only, preached during his last visit to the South Shore, were printed by A. Henry at *Halifax* in 1782 and 1783. The first, *A Sermon preached to and at the Request of a religious Society of young Men and engaged for the maintaining and enjoying of religious Worship in Liverpool, on the 19th of November 1782,* is a highly allegorical treatment of the resurrection story, and contains a clear exposition of Alline's criticisms of the current theories of the Atonement.
>
> The second sermon, also preached at Liverpool, *A Sermon on a Day of Thanksgiving . . . on the 21st of November, 1782,* is particularly valuable on account of the light it throws on the attitude of the "Yankee Neutrals" of Nova Scotia to the American Revolution.

Finally, *A Sermon Preached on the 19th of February 1783 at Fort-Midway,* was reprinted by Blunt and March at Newburyport, Massachusetts, in 1795 ... and again by S. Bragg Jr. at Dover, N.H., in 1797 ... The only explanation of the popularity of this sermon is the eloquence and emotionalism with which the goodness and love of God are presented.[24]

A few pages earlier in his book, Armstrong had referred to the "emotional fervor of Alline's preaching" to be found in his last published sermon. "Such highly charged emotionalism," Armstrong contended, "delivered in a fervent and eloquent manner, and accompanied no doubt with tears and sobs, was bound to have a tremendous effect upon his hearers."[25]

In his 1954 B.D. thesis "Henry Alline: Man of Conflict," completed at Acadia University, G. A. Morrison merely underscored, in a few well-chosen words, the points already made by Armstrong about Alline's sermons. Seventeen years later, J.M. Bumsted, in his *Henry Alline,*[26] was content to view Alline largely through his *Journal* and *The Anti-Traditionist.* It is noteworthy that out of a total of eighty-eight footnotes in this book only two are devoted to Alline's sermons, namely to the November 21, 1782 Liverpool sermon. Gordon Stewart, on the other hand, as has already been pointed out, buttressed his Ph.D. dissertation on Alline with scores of references to the three sermons. This emphasis also characterized the general approach taken in *A People Highly Favoured of God.*

In my own recent work on Alline, especially in *Ravished by the Spirit,* presented first in lecture format as the Hayward Lectures in 1983, and in my introduction to the *New Light Letters and Songs* (1983), I was remarkably silent about the sermons, stressing instead the central importance of the *Journal,* Alline's *Hymns and Spiritual Songs* and his *Anti-Traditionist.* I underplayed the significance of the sermons in these two books for one major reason. In 1982 and 1983 I was primarily interested in the impact of Alline's movement and theology on his followers in post-Revolutionary Nova Scotia, New Brunswick and New England. There seemed little need to add to my earlier assessment of Alline's impact on

13

Revolutionary Nova Scotia. Furthermore, my examination of what remained of the Allinite legacy in the New Brunswick-Nova Scotia-New England region during the half century or so after his death, unearthed limited interest in his sermons. On the other hand, his *Journal, Hymns and Spiritual Songs* and his *Anti-Traditionist*, or at least parts of the latter treatise, continued to have a considerable impact on the "Evangelical ethos" of the region well on into the nineteenth century.

Yet even though Alline's three published sermons may not throw much light on the evolving popular religious culture in the Maritimes and New England in the post-1784 period, they are of critical importance in understanding Alline's relationship with Nova Scotia's First Great Awakening. They tell us a great deal about Alline, the charismatic preacher, and why so many Nova Scotians resonated to his New Light message, and regarded him as "the Apostle of Nova Scotia."[27]

III

Little is known about how Alline's contemporaries actually responded to the three sermons which he eventually published. The only available eye-witness accounts are provided by Alline himself and by Simeon Perkins, the Liverpool merchant and civic leader. A perceptive and sensitive observer of the Liverpool religious scene, Perkins, while not a New Light enthusiast, was positive about Alline and his message. He described his sermons as "very Good,"[28] "very ingenious"[29] and his preaching as "Very Good"[30] and "Very Well."[31] In fact, Perkins did not write *one* negative word about Alline; the same cannot be said about Perkins's view of the Reverend Israel Cheever, Liverpool's alcoholic Congregational minister. On November 19, 1782, when Alline's *Sermon ... To ... Young Men* was preached, Perkins noted in his journal:

> Mr. Allen Preaches to the young People. When I came out of the meeting House, I discovered a Smack to rise from the Prize Brign.... Mr. Allen comes to See me & Lodges with me.[32]

Two days later, on November 21, Alline preached his Thanksgiving sermon to a huge congregation. According to Perkins:

> Thursday, Nov 21st — Wind Eastward. Thanksgiving day. Mr. Allan Preaches from Psalms, a very Good Discourse. Capt. Howard with his Officers and most of his men Attend. Proves Something wet, but the Soldiers work on the Barrack Chimneys.[33]

In his *Journal* account Alline said nothing specific about the November 19 and 21 Liverpool sermons. Instead, he recorded an evocative description of what he called "the glorious work of God."

> Almost all the town assembled together, and some that were lively christians prayed and exhorted, and God was there with a truth. I preached every day, and sometimes twice a day; and the houses where I went were crowded almost all the time. Many were brought out of darkness and rejoiced, and exhorted in public. And O how affecting it was to see some young people not only exhort their companions, but also take their parents by the hand, and entreat them for their soul's sake to rest no longer in their sins, but fly to Jesus Christ while there was hope. One young lad (who turned out to be a very bright christian) I saw, after sermon, take his father by the hand, and cry out, O father, you have been a great sinner, and now are an old man: an old sinner, with grey hairs upon your head, going right down to destruction. O turn, turn, dear father, return and fly to Jesus Christ: with many other such like expressions and entreaties, enough to melt a stony heart. The work of God continued with uncommon power through almost all the place. But the small number that did not fall in with the work were raging and scoffing, and some blaspheming.[34]

During late December, 1782, and much of January and early February 1783, Alline continued to pour oil on the revival fires. In early January he sailed to Halifax, with his two Liverpool manuscripts in his possession, and made

15

arrangements with the printer, A. Henry, to have them published. Alline detested Halifax, regarding Haligonians "in general . . . almost as dark and as vile as in Sodom."[35] After spending ten days in the Nova Scotia capital, Alline was delighted to return to Liverpool. Here he found — as he characteristically expressed it — "the waters troubled, and souls stepping in." He felt inspired to declare:

O the happy days which I there enjoyed, not only in my own soul, but to see the kingdom of God *flourishing*. When I went to preach at the meeting-house, at the hour appointed, the people were crowding to hear; and when the sermon was over, I was obliged to stop many hours in the broad-alley, to discourse with the people; for it seemed as if they could not go away. While I was there this last time, the christians gathered together in fellowship, by telling their experiences and getting fellowship one for another; and so joined in a body, separating themselves from the world.[36]

On Sunday, February 16, 1783, Alline preached his last sermons in Liverpool. Perkins's moving response sensitively reflected the response of his community:

Mr. Alline Preached both parts of the day & Evening. A Number of People made a Relation of their Experiences after the Meeting was concluded & Expressed Great Joy & Comfort in what god had done for them. Mr. Alline made a long Speech, Very Sensible, Advising all Sorts of People to a Religious Life, & gave many directions for their outward walk. This is a wonderfull day & Evening. Never did I behold Such an Appearance of the Spirit of God moving upon the people Since the time of the Great Religious Stir in New England many years ago.[37]

For Perkins, Alline's Revival had the same "Appearance" as New England's traumatic First Great Awakening. And it is clear that for Perkins and for most of his Nova Scotia Yankee contemporaries, Alline was carefully fitted into the Whitefieldian-Edwardsian Radical Evangelical framework. Alline's so-called heterodox views were never mentioned by

16

Perkins — only the "wonderful . . . Spirit of God moving upon the people." Other Nova Scotia Yankees would make precisely the same point. For example, Amos Hilton, a leading member of the Congregational Church in Yarmouth, when confronted by his anti-Alline minister, the Reverend Jonathan Scott, declared that a preacher's theology was really of secondary importance. "It was," Hilton replied to Scott's vicious critique of Alline's perceived heretical views, "no Matter of any great Consequence to him what a Man's Principles were, if he was but earnest in promoting a good Work."[38] As had been the case in New England's First Great Awakening "the manner in which a preacher delivered his message was often more revealing of his persuasion than the particular doctrines he happened to espouse."[39] In other words, preachers were viewed as being special instruments of the Almighty not because of the defensive religious orthodoxy they articulated but because they could trigger religious revivals into existence. The words uttered by the preacher were not nearly as important as the "New Birth" produced. Moreover, as the French writer La Rochfoucauld once perceptively observed: "Enthusiasm is the most convincing orator: it is like the functioning of an infallible law of nature. The simplest man, fired with enthusiasm, is more persuasive than the most eloquent without it."

On Monday, February 17, 1783, Alline made his way to Port Medway — (Fort-Midway or Port Midway or Portmetway) — a few miles to the northeast. He would never return to Liverpool. Perkins has nothing to say about the *Fort-Midway* sermon preached on February 19. All that Alline mentioned in his *Journal* was the following.

> February 17th.   I left Liverpool, stopped and preached at Port Miday, Petit-Riviere, Lehave and Malegash.
> 1.   O God, may I directed be,
>   While here, to follow none but thee.
>   Be this my theme, where'er I rove,
>   To tell the world of Jesus love
> 2.   Then when this mortal life shall cease,
>   I shall awake in realms of peace;
>   Where I with my dear God shall be;
>   And give the glory, Lord to thee.[40]

17

Realizing that he was dying of tuberculosis and still eager to share his sermons with posterity, Alline took with him to Halifax, late in February 1783, his Port Medway sermon. Henry published it sometime in the late spring. On August 27, determined "to blow . . . the gospel trump"[41] in New England, Alline sailed to his former home from Windsor. He had with him copies of all his published works — his three sermons, his *Two Mites, The Anti-Traditionist* and his tiny volume of *Hymns and Spiritual Songs.* Alline also carried with him his *Journal,* in shorthand, and some 500 of his hymns, still in manuscript form. After an unplanned stop at the mouth of the St. John River he reached northern Maine early in September. He died in New Hampshire on February 2, 1784.

IV

Simeon Perkins provides the only available contemporary eye-witness account of how any of Alline's published sermons may have impacted on the Liverpool region. Unfortunately for the historian, Perkins's responses are disconcertingly cryptic and brief. The same is true concerning more generalized contemporary reaction to Alline's preaching. At least three Nova Scotians, other than Perkins, positively affected by the revival, recorded their reactions to Alline's actual preaching. From their recorded reaction, it is clear that Alline must have indeed been a spellbinding preacher.

As late as 1856, for example, a ninety-three year old Mrs. Fox, a daughter of one of Alline's early converts — Benjamin Cleveland, the Horton hymn writer — could still vividly remember listening, as a teenager, to her first Christian sermon. It was preached by Alline in 1780. The sermon, she once observed, "made a deep impression on her mind;" seventy-six years after the event she could still recall Alline's text "John xii:35." It was observed that

> Mrs. Fox says she never heard Mr Alline preach but it
> warmed her heart; and she heard him very often. She
> used frequently to travel several miles to hear him; and
> never heard him without there being something fresh
> and new in his discourses.[42]

All of his sermons and his everyday discourse, she stressed, were "very spiritual." Alline "would not converse about the world at all, except as urged by necessity."[43]

Another woman from the region could never erase from her consciousness the vivid picture of Alline, deeply etched into her memory. Mary Coy Bradley in 1780 was only nine years old yet from her Massachusetts vantage-point in 1849 she could still hear, as if they had been preached yesterday, those remarkable sermons given by Alline to his Maugerville audience during the American Revolution. (Maugerville is located near Fredericton.) Bradley noted in her *Life and Christian Experiences:*

> In the 9th year of my age (1780), Mr Henry Allen, a New Light travelling minister came to preach. My parents took me with them twice to meeting. The first text was "And at midnight there was a cry made, Behold the Bridegroom cometh: go ye out to meet him." My attention was arrested, and for many days after I was engaged in ruminating and repeating over some parts of the sermon. The second time I heard him, the text was from Acts, second chapter, and three first verses . . .
>
> My mind was most affected from what he said about cloven tongues of fire, upon which he dwelt much in the latter part of his sermon. I imagined the house was full of cloven tongues, and I looked upon the heads of the people to see if I could not see them sitting upon each of them. I felt an awful dread but it brought no light nor understanding to my mind.[44]

Mary Coy Bradley also remembered that:

> After the sermon and worship was over, I was astonished to see the people talking and shaking hands, as I never before had witnessed. Some looked of a cheerful, loving, and happy countenance; others were in tears, and cast down.[45]

Three years earlier, in 1777, Handley Chipman, a leading craftsman and farmer from the Cornwallis, Nova Scotia area and father of Thomas Handley, one of Alline's early converts who was ordained in 1782, first heard Alline preach. Though criticized by many of his friends and associates, Chipman felt that the young New Light was indeed an instrument of the Almighty. He pointed out to two vociferous Presbyterian critics of Alline — the Reverends Daniel Cock and David Smith — that

> Since I have heard him and am acquainted with him I must acknowledge I like him very much and as we have no minister I cannot see any evil in hearing him preach, and this I am sure I never saw so many sin sick souls since I liv'd here as there now is and some near and dear to me and that caus'd I plainly see by God's belessing on Mr Allen's preaching and God forbid I should say it is the work of the devil.[46]

Chipman in 1777, it should be pointed out, was no impressionable teenager or immature nine-year-old. He was a well-read, highly regarded leader in his community. God was obviously "blessing" Alline's preaching and this, in the final analysis, according to Chipman, was the ultimate spiritual test. Throughout the remainder of his life he would never forget the way in which Alline used words as a "bare and brutal engine"[47] against the mind. Nor would many other Nova Scotians who had actually heard the Falmouth evangelist preach.[48]

V

It is known that Alline's three sermons were published by Anthony Henry, the Halifax printer, probably in 1782 and 1783. It is also known that only the *Fort-Midway* sermon was reprinted — first in 1795 and then in 1797. It was popular among the New England Free Will Baptists who used it, together with the *Anti-Traditionist* and Alline's *Hymns and Spiritual Songs*, in the last decades of the 18th century, to attack their Calvinist foes. It is ironic that Alline's hymnody and Free Will theology, together with his "Neo-Whitefieldian" preaching style, did possibly exert a greater influence in post Revolutionary New England than in post-Revolutionary Nova Scotia and New Brunswick.

Part of the *Fort-Midway* sermon would also be reprinted in the United States in 1975 — this time not by the

Free Will Baptists but by *Decision* a monthly periodical published by the Billy Graham Evangelistic Association.[49] The editor of *Decision*, Sherwood Wirt, had in early 1975 read *A People Highly Favoured of God*. As a result, Wirt decided that one of Alline's sermons — "preferably an evangelistic sermon" — be included in "*Decision* magazine at an early date."[50] Wirt decided to use the 1795 *A Gospel Call to Sinners* version of the *Fort-Midway* sermon but retitled it "I Seek My Brethren." The article was introduced with one sentence: "Canadians will never forget the preacher who brought the Great Awakening to Nova Scotia with messages like this one preached at Fort-Midway in 1783."[51] Only the last five pages of the sermon were, in fact, used and these were heavily edited. I am sure that no one noticed the difference and no one really cared. For, despite Dr. Wirt's 1975 claim, most Canadians had long before forgotten Alline. If anything, Americans were, and had been, more interested in Alline than had been Canadians, even those from New Brunswick and Nova Scotia.

VI

Alline's New Light message and theology had at its core what has been referred to as "the distinctive elements of the Evangelical tradition . . . intense conversion experience, fervid piety, ecstatic worship forms, Biblical literalism, the pure church ideal, and charismatic leadership."[52] And as far as Alline was concerned, "intense conversion experience" — what he referred to over and over again, as "the ravishing of the soul"[53] — was of the greatest importance in any litany of crucial characteristics of the Radical Evangelical style. Alline's own traumatic conversion was, without question, the critically important event of his life and provided the driving thrust to his preaching. His spiritual transformation provided the pattern for his hearers, first to appropriate and then to impose upon others. The Falmouth evangelist had no difficulty in generalizing from the experience of his own particular conversion and making it the universally accepted evangelical norm. If Alline could experience "the infinite condescension of God"[54] and be marvellously "ravished with divine ectasy

21

beyond any doubts" and be "wrapped up in God,"[55] so could any inhabitant of the colony. All they needed to do was to reach out to the Almighty, as Alline had done in the early months of 1775, and be "willing to be redeemed."[56]

For Alline the Scriptures and his own conversion experience had convincingly shown that Calvinism as preached in Nova Scotia was a pernicious heresy. "The lesson, why those, that are lost, are not redeemed," he argued, "is not because that God delighted in their Misery, or by any Neglect in God, God forbid." Rather, it resulted "by the Will of the Creature; which, instead of consenting to Redeeming Love, rejects it, and therefore cannot possibly be redeemed." "Men and Devils," he asserted, and this would be the bedrock theological position to be found in all of his written work, "that are miserable are not only the author of their own Misery," but they also act "against the Will of God, the Nature of God, and the most endearing Expression of his Love."[57]

Influenced to an extent by English writers such as William Law, John Fletcher, Edward Young and John Milton, but most significantly by his own conversion, Alline was determined to attack Calvinism root and branch. One of the critical intellectual and spiritual problems he faced, right from the beginning, was how "to account for the presence of sin and evil in a universe which was supposedly the handiwork of a benevolent and almighty Creator."[58] Alline did so by emphasizing, as Law had done, that the world was not created "out of nothing." A contemporary critic of Alline's theology, Hannah Adams of Boston, perceptively described in 1785 his "Out-birth" thesis:

> that the souls of all the human race are emanations, or rather parts of one Great Spirit; but that they individually originally had the powers of moral agents; that they were all present with our first parents in Eden, and were actual in the first transgression. He supposes, that our first parents in innocency were pure spirits, without material bodies; that the material world was not then made; but in some consequence of the fall man being cut off from God, that they might not sink into immediate destruction, the world was produced, and then clothed with hard bodies, and that all the human

race will in their turns, by natural regeneration, be invested with such bodies, and in them enjoy a state of probation for happiness of immortal duration.[59]

For Alline, men, as "emanations" of the "One Great Spirit," shared the Almighty's "immortal Power of thought" and also the Almighty's "immortal Cloathing or Outbirth." Thus, according to Alline, not only Adam, but all mankind existed in this pristine pre-material state — "an innumerable Throng of angellic Beings, brought forth in this glorious System." All mankind were originally spiritual beings, existing in spiritual "Vessels, floating in a limitless spiritual universe." It was "a paradisical System" where all mankind was able "to bask in the boundless Ocean of their Father's Love and Perfections."[60]

Then sin appeared — not because of some Divine decree or Adam's sin — but because man was made in the image of God and shared fully "in the freedom of choice and of will which is part of the divine nature."[61] All mankind, and not only Adam, began

> to view the Beauty and Grandeur of his outward Creature; which pleasing Thought of his own Grandeur began to draw his Attention, and cause him to fall in love with his paradisical Clothing; so that of Consequence the inward Creature or Power of Choice turned from the only Spring of Life into his own Clothing, and therefore his will not only turned, but began to increase that way.[62]

Thus for Alline each and every human being has "actually and consciously participated in the first sin."[63] This theory became reality at the moment of regeneration when, according to Alline, "you will certainly remember your Rebellion in the Garden of Eden, as any Sin that you ever committed, yea, and as clearly as the Man remembers his past conduct, when he awakes out of his sleep."[64]

For Alline, there was no spiritual basis for the doctrine of predestination. God did not predestine anyone to salvation or damnation. Nor was there any such thing as "Original Sin" imputed to all mankind by Adam. "You have no more Reason to say," Alline once observed, "that Adam's Sin was imputed to you, than he has to complain and say, that your Sin was imputed to him."[65] Relentless in his attack on the underpinnings of predestination, and determined to persuade his hearers of the efficacy of "free grace, free grace,"[66] Alline stressed the importance of each individual's choosing freely to return to his or her "paradisical state." This could only be done if the "spiritual and immortal . . . Mind," found "in everyone," was presented to the "Son of God" leaving behind "the fallen immortal Body in its fallen State still."[67] For, according to Alline, the "New Birth" was "that Moment" when "the Will and Choice was turned after God" and the regenerate "acted with God, and therefore partake of God; and thus again brought to enjoy the Tree of Life, which they had lost; and are reinstated in that Paradise that they fell out of."[68]

Since, for Alline, each individual was free and capable of "consenting to Redeeming Love," he felt it necessary to trace in as simple terms as possible the actual pattern of the "New Birth" process. Conviction, "bringing the Sinner to a Sense of his fallen, helpless and deplorable condition" — of falling into a state of eternal separation from "The Triune God" — was, he had to admit, sometimes a gradual process. Nevertheless, he asserted that "the Work of conversion is instantaneous."[69]

The convicted sinner, as far as Alline was concerned, felt both drawn to and repelled by the Almighty. The now completely disoriented individual

> sees that to fly from his Guilt and Misery is impracticable: and to reform or make Satisfaction, as much impossible; and therefore like the four Lepers at the Gates of Samaria (2 Kings 7:3, 4) he is determined to try the last Remedy; for to stay where he is, is certain Death, and to return back unto his former State of Security, will be Death, and therefore, altho' he cannot see, that Christ has any love for him, or Pity towards him; neither doth he see, whether He intends to have Mercy on him or not; yet he is determined to cast himself at his Feet, and trust wholly to his Mercy, and Free Grace for Salvation; and cries out with the trembling Leper. *Lord if thou wilt* (Mark 1:40)[70]

And the merciful, loving God always answers yes not because of some obsession with substitutionary atonement but because Christ "dies to lift a Dying World While Love Doth graft them on the tree of Life."[71] By having his perfect life squeezed from him because of the weight of human sin — not as a sacrifice to his Father — Christ enables everyone to return to their original home in "the Mansions of Delight."[72]

At that precise moment when the convicted individual "is willing to be redeemed out of his fallen state on the Gospel-Terms," then "the Redeeming Love enters into his soul" as Christ "the hope of Glory takes possession of the inner man." The ravished souls find "the Burden of Their Sin gone, with their Affections taken off this World, and set on things above." Moreover, "their Hearts" were "drawn out after Christ, under a feeling sense of the Worth of his Redeeming Love; at the same Time with a sense of their own Vileness, and the Vanity of all things here below, together with the worth and Sweetness of heavenly Things, and the Amiableness of the Divine Being."[73]

Despite this anti-Calvinism, and possibly because of it, Alline declared that there was indeed a "final Perseverance of the Saints." Of course, as long as one lived on earth, there would be, as Alline himself had painfully experienced, an often bitter struggle between the sanctified "inmost Soul" and the "fallen immortal Body." Yet because of his dualism, and his emphasis on the centrality of the "ravishing of the soul by Christ," Alline found himself asserting that "that which is born of God cannot sin."[74]

Realizing the threat posed to his theological system by Antinomianism, Alline carefully balanced his emphasis on "perseverance" with what has been accurately referred to as a powerful "asceticism and bodily mortification worthy of the most austere monasticism."[75] In *Two Mites*, for example, and also in his sermons, he would maintain that "True redemption is raising the desires and life of the inner man out of this miserable, sinful, and bestial world, and turning it to Christ, from whence it is fallen."[76] To be a Christian was to be like Christ — radically different from "the world." In *The Anti-Traditionist*, Alline felt compelled to stress that it was incumbent upon the truly redeemed to "Turn from all, Deny all: Leave all." He went on:

I do not mean the outward and criminal Acts of Idolatry and Debauchery only: but any and every Thing in the Creature that in the least Degree amuses the Mind or leads the Choice from God. For even the most simple Enjoyments and Pleasures of Life will keep the Choice in Action, and therefore the Creatures amused from God, and consequently sinking deeper and deeper in its fallen and irrevocable State. Nor will you ever return to be redeemed until every Idol, Joy, Hope, or Amusement so fails you that you are wholly starved out, and there is not only a Famine, but a mighty Famine in all created Good.[77]

Carefully blended, Alline's "perseverance of the spiritually ravished saints" and his introspective asceticism produced what he once called "true zeal."[78] "Perseverance" without "asceticism," he knew all too well, would lead directly to the evils of Calvinist Antinomianism which he had so vehemently denounced. The latter without the former, he knew, was mere hypocricy. Alline would carefully weave these two themes through his sermons, producing in the process the impression that not only was he a special instrument of the Almighty — Nova Scotia's John the Baptist preparing the way for the Lord — but also the articulator of the Radical Evangelicalism of George Whitefield and Jonathan Edwards. There was, despite his many unorthodox views, in Alline's message what has been called an Orthodox "Whitefieldian sound."[79] Alline, in other words, *sounded* like a New England New Light from the 1740's. His dynamic and charismatic preaching produced many of the same results. Moreover, and this point needs to be emphasized, the Falmouth evangelist intuitively realized that his New Light movement, without his careful nurturing, would fragment into warring Antinomian and anti-Antinomian factions.

There is certainly a ring of truth in John Wesley's contention that in Alline's message "the gold and dross" were "shuffled together."[80] This theme was developed further in a particularly discerning critique put forward by the Reverend Matthew Richey — a key Methodist leader. For Richey, Alline's "tenets were a singular combination of heterogeneous

26

materials derived from opposite sources." And as far as the Methodist leader was concerned,

> They were fragments of different systems — without coherence, and without any mutual relation or dependence. With the strong assertion of man's freedom as a moral agent, he connected the doctrine of the final perseverance of the saints. He allegorized to such excess the plainest narratives and announcements of Scriptures, that the obvious and unsophisticated import of the words of inspiration was often entirely lost amidst the reveries of mysticism.[81]

Alline had always made it quite clear that the "scriptures are not to be understood in their literal sense, but have a spiritual meaning."[82] He tried to make each verse in the Bible speak directly and profoundly to each of his listeners — as throbbing thrusts of spirituality. He shattered the hard outer case of Calvinist orthodoxy in order to enable "divine ectasy" to "ravish" the collective soul of Nova Scotia and New England. In the process, he abandoned the central convictions of Evangelical Christianity, such as the Creation, the Atonement, the Resurrection of the body, the Sacraments, and the authority of the Bible. Instead, driven by the inner compelling logic of his own profound conversion, and by his conviction that he was in direct communication with the Almighty, he pushed the parameters of experiential religion to, and some would say beyond, the most radical Evangelical norms. And some of his followers pushed his views into a particularly virulent Nova Scotia and New Brunswick variant of Antinomianism.[83] If he had been alive, Alline would have been both humiliated and incensed by this anti-Christian "vanity and sin."[84] Yet he should have realized that it would be extremely difficult, if not impossible, for many of his followers to walk his knife-edge of "true zeal."

VII

Alline's sermons must be viewed in the context of his times, his theology and his own personality. They must also be examined as sermons — as three extant sermons from the more than 1,000 sermons that Alline extemporaneously preached during his lifetime. He undoubtedly used many of the same points raised in these three sermons and much of the actual language in many of the other sermons that he preached as he crisscrossed Nova Scotia from 1777 to 1783. Alline did not have the time to prepare sermons; he preached as the Spirit moved him. He soon learned how to affect his listeners positively. He used language they could understand — earthy, sexual, simple, evocative and often powerful. He instinctively knew how to link words together to create literary images which drilled into the human mind, first transforming doubt into agory, and then agony into intense spiritual relief. For Alline, as had been the case for Augustine centuries earlier, effective preaching was the "ministry of the tongue" whereby the preacher "succeeded in putting Christ in the worshipper's ears." Sometimes his preaching, "charged with emotionalism," delivered in a "fervent and eloquent manner" in a resonating tenor voice, became superb poetry.[85] Sometimes, the poetry was sung as a spiritual song which was then immediately followed by an almost frenzied outburst of words directed at specific people in his audience. This too was an important characteristic of Alline's preaching. He loved to direct certain themes in his sermons at certain people — at the young, at the old, at the fishermen, at the community leaders, at the soldiers. People who heard Alline must have felt that he was preaching especially to them, and hundreds positively responded to this form of directed intimacy.

It is not surprising that Jonathan Scott bitterly complained that Alline's books and sermons were "interspersed with Poetry calculated to excite and raise the Passions of the Reader, especially the young, ignorant and inconsistent, who are influenced more by the Sound and Gingle of the words, then by solid Sentences and rational and scriptural Ideas of divine and eternal Things; and hereby are prepared to take in, and embrace all the destructive and Religion-destroying and Soul-destroying Sentiments

28

is that why he failed?

contained therein."[86] Scott's observation tells us why Alline was such a success in Nova Scotia, and Scott such a failure. Alline appealed to the "Passions," especially of the young, Scott to the head — to the "rational." Alline articulated the novel, the experiential while Scott mouthed orthodox shibboleths. Alline's preaching triggered a widespread revival; Scott's "solid" and "rational" preaching resulted in indifference and spiritual apathy. Scott seemed to point back to an increasingly irrelevant Calvinist past; Alline, on the other hand, appeared to thrust his listeners into the future — a future promising "individual liberty" and eternal hope. One of Alline's popular hymns made the point in this way:

> And Hail a Brighter Morning near
> When Heavens great Sun Shall once appear
> All Suns and Stars Shall Cease to Shine
> But this Eternal Sun of Mine
>
> Far, Far, from interposing Night
> Awake in Uncreated Light
> My raptured Soul with all the throng
> Shall Join in Heavens immortal Song[87]

Scott may have been, while in southern Nova Scotia, a failure as a preacher and pastor. He was, however, an astute and caustic critic of Alline and his theology. In *A Brief View of the Religious Tenets and Sentiments . . . of Mr Henry Alline*, published in Halifax in the summer of 1784, Scott aimed specifically at *Two Mites, The Anti-Traditionist* and the November 19, 1782, Liverpool *Sermon*. Scott not only presented a "faithful picture. . . of Puritan orthodoxy as it was preached in Nova Scotia,"[88] but he also convincingly showed how successful Alline had been in destroying Calvinist "Tradition and Order."[89]

Scott devoted twenty pages of *A Brief View*, "Section XIII," to Alline's Liverpool *Sermon*.[90] It is the only available contemporary critique of the *Sermon* and, without question, the most detailed ever written. "Section XIII" is reprinted in its entirety as Appendix I of this volume. It is noteworthy that Scott concentrated on what he regarded as Alline's heretical interpretation of the Scriptures, of the Atonement, and of the

29

Incarnation. Yet, he also had to admit that Alline's view of conversion was indeed virtually the same as the Orthodox New England Evangelical version. "Our Author," Scott maintained, "allows of no Imputation of the Righteousness of Christ to Sinners, 'but the pure Spirit of Christ in them;' in which Expressions he confounds, or rather wholly excludes Justification by Faith in the Righteousness of Christ, while he is teaching the Infusion of Grace into the Soul in Regeneration and Sanctification." Then Scott concludes:

> But we must not give up the Doctrine of Justification by the Righteousness of Christ imputed, to make Way for the Doctrine of Regeneration and Sanctification by the holy Spirit, seeing both as taught with great Plainess, and the former as well as the latter in the holy Scriptures; and have a perfect Consistence and Agreement with each other: And as Things are constituted, the former is as absolutely necessary and essential to our Salvation, as the latter.[91]

Alline would have probably replied that his half a loaf was infinitely better than Scott's whole loaf.

VIII

Why was Alline such a successful preacher? A variety of answers have already been provided. He was successful, it has been argued, because his "Radical Evangelical" message provided answers to disoriented and confused Nova Scotians desperately looking for meaning in life. His message was widely regarded as infused by charismatic power. It was felt that he was an inspired instrument of the Almighty not only because he said that he was but also because his preaching resulted in conversions, many of them. The reasoning might have been circuitous yet it was also convincing to his contemporaries. There was a widespread revival in Nova Scotia. Alline was the key evangelist in the revival. And hence Alline's preaching was the means whereby the Holy Spirit swept across the colony.[92]

It should be remembered that in his preaching Alline emphasized the fact that he was in direct communication with the Almighty who inspired his every word and every action. Not only had he experienced God directly through "the scriptures," not only had he actually heard "the still small voice" of God, but he had also, for what seemed to be an eternal moment, actually seen the Almighty. At all levels of sensory experience, Alline had been overwhelmed by the divine presence which had penetrated the deepest recesses of his being.[93] It is not surprising, therefore, that when he preached, Alline underscored the fact that he was indeed a special intermediary between God and his fellow Nova Scotians and New Englanders. "The Lord," Alline frequently informed his receptive hearers, "is come with a stammering tongue, to seek you."[94]

Christ evidently spoke to Nova Scotians by Alline's "stammering tongue." Alline's heretical views and his anti-Calvinism did little to disuade the thousands who flocked to hear "that man of God"[95] from their conviction that Alline possessed divine and supernatural sanction and power. He succeeded in juxtaposing fear and anxiety with love and security. Yet the question must be asked: why was Alline's "Free Grace" gospel so readily accepted in those areas of the colony where Calvinism had hitherto been widely regarded as the orthodox norm? Did Alline, almost single-handedly, shatter the old Calvinist hegemony over Yankee Nova Scotia? According to Maurice Armstrong this is precisely what he did. Alline's mystical pietism helped to transform the Calvinist-Puritan obsession with order and deference into a "growing appreciation of the dignity and rights of man," and of the crucial importance "of personal and political freedom."[96] Armstrong's assertion, unfortunately is not supported by any references to the Nova Scotia situation, either during, or after the Awakening. Moreover, Armstrong does not try to develop his argument that Alline's revival was Nova Scotia's American Revolution and the means whereby the foundations of Calvinism were, once and for all, completely undermined.

In the short run Alline certainly weakened Calvinism's hold on Yankee Nova Scotia. But it should never be forgotten that he refused to abandon a key theological construct of Calvinism, the perseverance of the saints. This may help to explain why people who might regard themselves as orthodox

31

[handwritten annotation: Key to appeal of all in Antinomian Strain]

Calvinists, could still accept his message. Alline's emphasis on "Free Grace" meant that at the human side of the cosmic equation, there would be certainty — a certainty that could never be provided by Calvinism and predestination. In the late 1770's and early 1780's, many people in Nova Scotia were looking for a religious experience which they could themselves trigger. Alline's preaching obviously provided this. But they were also looking for Calvinist assurance. In a sense, Alline provided them with the best of both worlds: they edged into a nineteenth-century Arminian future yet could look back to their Puritan Calvinist past in seventeenth-century New England.

That Alline's "Free Grace" gospel did *not*, in fact, destroy Calvinism in Nova Scotia in the long run is convincingly demonstrated by the history of the Baptist movement in the province.[97] The Baptists considered themselves in the post 1800 period to be the inheritors of Alline's New Light tradition. The Baptist majority in Nova Scotia, led by such early disciples of Alline as Thomas Handley Chipman, Edward and James Manning, Joseph Dimock, among others, moved their denomination toward Calvinist order and away from Alline's New Light Free Grace. There would be ardent advocates of the Allinite position within the Baptist tradition in Nova Scotia but they would find themselves a rather insignificant minority. In neighbouring New Brunswick, on the other hand, as the nineteenth century unfolded, the Allinite-Free Will component of the burgeoning Baptist movement was much larger and more influential than in Nova Scotia. In the census of 1871, for example, out of a total Nova Scotia population of 387,800, there were 54,263 "Regular" (Calvinist) Baptists, 14.0% of the population, and 19,032 "Free" Baptists, or 4.9% of the total population. In New Brunswick, on the other hand, out of a population of 285,594 there were 42,729 "Regular" Baptists, 15.0% of the population, and 27,866 "Free" Baptists, 9.8% of all New Brunswickers.[98] As David Bell has persuasively argued, it was ironic that Henry Alline should have a greater long term impact on New Brunswick — the Loyalist Province, created the year of his death — than in his home province of Nova Scotia.[99]

32

IX

The following sermons of Henry Alline speak for themselves. They convincingly show that, as the Methodist *Book of Discipline* put it, Alline used in his preaching style "the best general method." According to the *Discipline*, effective Evangelical preaching had "1. To convince: 2. To offer Christ: 3. To invite: 4. To build up: And to do this in some measure in every sermon."[100] Although not a Methodist, Alline was certainly very much a Methodist in the way he preached.

Alline's sermons also convincingly show both his remarkable strengths as a preacher, and some of his theological flaws. In my view, they merit reprinting because of their historical importance, but not for that reason only. They also possess considerable contemporary relevance. Alline's world, in so many ways, was very different from our own. Yet it was also, in a certain spiritual sense, very similar. In our day, the sermons may in the 1980's be read at two levels. Most will read them as curious historical documents from a confused and confusing distant past. A few readers, however, might see in the sometimes opaque and obtuse pages a few amazingly penetrating and creative insights. Alline, I am sure, would perceive the reprinting of the three sermons as simply taking place in what he referred to and underscored as the "ONE ETERNAL NOW." As far as the Falmouth evangelist was concerned, there was no "Time and Space and successive Periods."[101] "With God," he argued, "there is neither Succession nor Progress; but that with Him the Moment He said let us make Man, and the Sound of the last Trumpet, is the very same instant, and your Death as much first as your Birth . . . with God all things are NOW . . . as the Center of a Ring, which is as near the one side as the other."[102] Alline's "ONE ETERNAL NOW" telescopes the Liverpool region of 1782 and 1783 into Nova Scotia of to-day and to-morrow. Alline's sermons are, in other words, "NOW" being preached. If the imagination could permit such a collapsing of time, the jagged edges of memory and immediacy which were felt by Alline's contemporaries, could perhaps be experienced by readers to-day. We, too, could walk the tight-rope between extreme immanence and radical transcendance. Perhaps not. And should the historian even consider such a possibility?

33

NOTES:

1. D. Bell, "All Things New: The Transformation of Maritime Baptist Historiography," *Nova Scotia Historical Review* (Vol. 4, No. 2, 1984), p. 81.

2. *Ibid.*

3. See, for example, the brief discussion of this problem in the introduction by James Beverley and Barry Moody to their edition of *The Life and Journal of The Rev. Mr. Henry Alline* (Hantsport, 1982), pp. 11-12. See also Bell, "All Things New."

4. D.G. Bell (ed), *Newlight Baptist Journals of James Manning and James Innis* (Hantsport, 1984), p. xiii. For Bell, Alline "stands unrivalled as the greatest 'Canadian' of the eighteenth century, the greatest Maritimer of any age and the most significant religious figure this country has yet produced."

5. From an "Extract of a Letter from John Allan," Sept. 22, 1777, quoted in Gordon Stewart and G.A. Rawlyk, *A People Highly Favoured of God* (Toronto, 1972), p. 75.

6. See my *Ravished by the Spirit* (Montreal, 1984), p. 9.

7. This point was first developed in Gordon Stewart's Ph.D. thesis, "Religion and the Yankee Mind of Nova Scotia during the American Revolution" (Queen's University, 1971). See also, G. Stewart and G. Rawlyk, *A People Highly Favoured of God* (Toronto, 1972).

8. H. Alline, *Two Mites on Some of the Most Important and Much Disputed Points of Divinity. . .* (Halifax, 1781), p. 234.

9. This theme is developed in much greater detail in Stewart, "Religion and the Yankee Mind," and also in Stewart and Rawlyk, *A People Highly Favoured of God.* The central thrust of this argument was first developed in G. Rawlyk and G. Stewart, "Nova Scotia's

Sense of Mission," in *Social History/Histoire Sociale*, II (1968), pp. 5-17. For a criticism of this thesis see J. Bumsted, *Henry Alline, 1748-84* (Toronto, 1971), pp. 51-74 and Beverley and Moody, *The Journal of Henry Alline*, pp. 12-13.

10. G. A. Rawlyk, "Henry Alline and the Canadian Baptist Tradition," The McMaster Divinity College *Theological Bulletin*, Vol. IV, No. 4 (June, 1977), p. 6.

11. Beverley and Moody, *The Journal of Henry Alline*, p. 220.

12. See E.L. Tuveson, *Redeemer Nation: The Idea of America's Millenial Role* (Chicago, 1968).

13. M. Armstrong, *The Great Awakening in Nova Scotia* (Hartford, 1948), p. 92.

14. G. Patterson, *Memoir of the Rev. James McGregor* (Philadelphia, 1859), p. 351.

15. Armstrong, *The Great Awakening*, p. 92.

16. See my discussion of this point in *Ravished by the Spirit*, pp. 13-14.

17. For a more detailed treatment of the importance Alline's hymns and spiritual songs see M. Filshie, "Redeeming Love Shall Be Our Song: Hymns of The First Great Awakening in Nova Scotia," (unpublished M.A. thesis, Queen's University, 1983) and G.A. Rawlyk (ed), *New Light Letters and Songs* (Hantsport, 1983), pp. 16-22, 183-246.

18. S.A. Marini, "New England Folk Religions, 1770-1815: The Sectarian Impulse in Revolutionary Society" (Ph.D. Dissertation, Harvard University, 1978), p. 2. This thesis, much revised, was published under the title *Radical Sects of Revolutionary New England* (Cambridge, 1982).

19. D.D. Bruce, Jr., *And They All Sang Hallelujah, Plain-Folk Camp Meeting Religion, 1800-1845* (Knoxville, 1975), p. 95.

20. (Toronto, 1982).

21. (Kingston, 1982). This slim volume was privately printed.

22. See Stewart's "Religion and the Yankee Mind."

23. (Toronto, 1948).

24. Armstrong, *The Great Awakening in Nova Scotia*, p. 93.

25. *Ibid.*, p. 82.

26. (Toronto, 1971).

27. Armstrong, *The Great Awakening in Nova Scotia*, p. 86. On Alline's New Hampshire tombstone the following sentence was added to the original inscription: "He was a burning and a shining light and justly esteemed the Apostle of Nova Scotia."

28. D.C. Harvey and C.B. Fergusson (eds), *The Diary of Simeon Perkins 1780-1789*, Vol. II (Toronto, 1958), p. 169.

29. *Ibid.*, p. 168.

30. *Ibid.*, p. 172.

31. *Ibid.*, p. 174.

32. *Ibid.*, p. 169.

33. *Ibid.*

34. Beverley and Moody, *The Journal of Henry Alline*, pp. 208-209.

35. *Ibid.*, p. 210.

36. *Ibid.*

37. Harvey and Fergusson, *The Diary of Simeon Perkins 1780-1789*, p. 177.

38. P.A.N.S. "Records of the Church of Jebogue in Yarmouth," p. 140.

39. A. Heimert, *Religion and the American Mind from the Great Awakening to the Revolution* (Cambridge, 1966), p. 169.

40. Beverley and Moody, *The Journal of Henry Alline*, p. 210.

41. *Ibid.*, p. 214.

42. J. Davis, *Life and Times of the Late Rev. Harris Harding, Yarmouth, N.S.* (Charlottetown, 1866), p. 187.

43. *Ibid.*

44. Mary Coy Bradley, *The Life and Christian Experiences of Mrs. Mary Bradley* (Boston, 1849), p. 16.

45. *Ibid.*, p. 16. The manuscript "Reminiscences of Mrs. Mary Bradley," located at the New England Historical and Genealogical Society, Boston, Massachusetts, is very similar to her *The Life and Christian Experiences.* For a further discussion of the "Reminiscences" see Bell, *Newlight Baptist Journals*, pp. 132-133.

46. P.A.N.S. Patterson Scrapbook, H. Chipman to Messrs. Cock and Smith, June 30, 1777. See the other interesting Chipman materials to be found in the P.A.N.S.

47. See. P. Miller, *Errand into the Wilderness* (Cambridge, 1964), p. 167.

48. I have now read scores of obituaries of Nova Scotians who died in the first half of the 19th century but who, to their dying day, remembered how Henry Alline had, in some special way, touched their lives. Some would remember a prayer, others some "spiritual conversation," a few his singing, and some others would merely refer to his preaching in a general way. What this

suggests to me is that Alline's preaching, broadly defined, resonated with his listeners. They heard him and listened to him because he was telling them something that struck a responsive chord deep in the inner recesses of their "minds and hearts." For a further discussion of this theme see my *Ravished by the Spirit*, pp. 44-34.

49. *Decision* (August, 1975), p. 4.

50. See M. Weasler to Gordon Stewart, Feb. 28, 1975. Letter in possession of G.A. Rawlyk.

51. *Decision* (August, 1975), p. 4.

52. Marini, "New England Folk Religions," p. 20.

53. See my discussion of this point in *Ravished by the Spirit*, p. 5.

54. Beverley and Moody, *The Journal of Henry Alline*, p. 63.

55. *Ibid.*

56. *Ibid.*, pp. 60-64.

57. Alline, *Two Mites*, pp. 150-1.

58. Armstrong, *The Great Awakening in Nova Scotia*, pp. 95-6.

59. H. Adams, *Alphabetical Compendium of the Various Sects which have Appeared in the World* (Boston, 1784), pp. lxiv-lxv.

60. Alline. *The Anti-Traditionist*, pp. 24-5.

61. Armstrong, *The Great Awakening in Nova Scotia*, p. 97.

62. Alline. *The Anti-Traditionist*, p. 31.

63. Armstrong, *The Great Awakening in Nova Scotia*, p. 98.

64. Alline, *The Anti-Traditionist*, pp. 24-5.

65. *Ibid.*, p. 25.

66. Beverley and Moody, *The Journal of Henry Alline*, p. 63.

67. Alline, *Two Mites*, p. 94.

68. Alline, *The Anti-Traditionist*, p. 40.

69. See *Two Mites*, pp. 121-135 for a detailed description of the "morphology of conversion."

70. *Ibid.*, p. 126.

71. Alline, *The Anti-Traditionist*, p. 34.

72. *Ibid.*, p. 54.

73. Alline, *Two Mites*, pp. 128-9.

74. *Ibid.*, p. 95.

75. Armstrong, *The Great Awakening in Nova Scotia*, p. 101.

76. Alline, *Two Mites*, p. 93.

77. Alline, *The Anti-Traditionist*, p. 42.

78. Beverley and Moody, *The Journal of Henry Alline*, p. 216.

79. See the discussion of this point in S. Marini, *Radical Sects of Revolutionary New England* and Rawlyk, *Ravished by the Spirit*. See also J.B. Bowles, *The Great Revival 1787-1805: The Origins of the Southern Evangelical Mind* (Lexington, 1972).

80. John Wesley to William Black, July 13, 1783 in J. Telford (ed), *The Letters of the Rev. John Wesley*, Vol. VII (London, 1931), pp. 182-3. The Nova Scotia Methodists, led by men like William Black and Freeborn Garrettson, were in the 1780's particularly

critical of Alline's theology as, of course, was the Reverend Jonathan Scott. In the post-1784 period, Anglican, Presbyterian and Baptist critics would join the Methodist anti-Alline chorus.

81. M. Richey, *A Memoir of the Late Rev. William Black* (Halifax, 1839), p. 45.

82. Adams, *Alphabetical Compendium*, p. lxv.

83. See Rawlyk, *New Light Letters and Songs*, pp. 37-66 and Bell, *Newlight Baptist Journals*, pp. 14-19, 337-354.

84. Beverley and Moody, *The Journal of Henry Alline*, p. 216.

85. Armstrong, *The Great Awakening in Nova Scotia*, p. 82.

86. Scott, *Brief View*, p. 168.

87. Quoted in Rawlyk, *New Light Letters and Songs*, p. 218.

88. Armstrong, *The Great Awakening in Nova Scotia*, p. 105.

89. See, for example, Scott, *Two Mites*, pp. 255-257.

90. *Ibid.*, pp. 169-189.

91. Scott, *Two Mites*, p. 188.

92. See Stewart and Rawlyk, *A People Highly Favoured of God*, pp. 45-76. See also Gordon Stewart's important article, "Charisma and Integration: an Eighteenth Century North American Case," *Comparative Studies in Society and History*, XVI (1974), pp. 138-149.

93. See, for example, Alline's description of his conversion in Beverley and Moody, *The Journal of Henry Alline*, pp. 60-66.

94. H. Alline, *A Gospel Call to Sinners* (Newburyport, 1795), p. 29.

95. See, for example, the description of Edward Manning's conversion in his "Reminiscences" (Acadia University Archives, Manning Papers). Many other examples may also be provided from conversion narratives to be found in various nineteenth century Maritime Baptist periodicals.

96. Armstrong, *The Great Awakening in Nova Scotia*, p. 105. S.D. Clark was not interested in the undermining of Calvinism. Instead he stressed the disintegration of the Congregational Church in Nova Scotia because of what he calls "Ecological, cultural and political" reasons and the "greater flexibility" of Alline's New Light movement. See Clark, *Church and Sect*, p. 36.

97. I have developed this theme at some length in my *Ravished by the Spirit*; see especially pp. 74-104.

98. See *ibid.*, p. 171.

99. Bell, *Newlight Baptist Journals*, pp. 22-35.

100. Quoted in Bowles, *The Great Revival*, p. 112. There is in this study an especially important chapter entitled "Homiletics & Hymnology," pp. 111-124. Much of what Bowles writes about Southern Evangelical culture could also be applied to Nova Scotia.

101. Alline, *The Anti-Traditionist*, pp. 62-3.

102. Alline, *Two Mites*, pp. 20-21.

SERMON

PREACHED TO,
AND AT THE REQUEST,
OF A RELIGIOUS SOCIETY OF
YOUNG MEN

UNITED AND ENGAGED FOR THE
MAINTAINING AND ENJOYING OF
RELIGIOUS WORSHIP
IN LIVERPOOL
On the 19th November, 1782.

By HENRY ALLINE

Printed by A. Henry.

DEAR BRETHREN.

ALTHOUGH it may be accounted arrogancy in me, yet I must omit that too common apology that preface most Books *"It was not my will, nor design, but the strong sollicitations of others introduced those lines to the publick.* For God forbid, that I should either preach or write any thing but what I would with joy and the greatest Delight spread (if possible) over the four quarters of the globe; and therefore with much satisfaction I answer your request not only rejoicing to find you possessed of such a godly zeal for the truths of the everlasting gospel: But likewise under a hope that God may make them of further benefit to your own souls (when I am far absent from you or cold in death) and likewise spread their usefullness where perhaps my voice may never be heard. And O should the spirit of God by these few lines hand one immortal soul to Jesus far more to you and me than all the applause of men, and dust of Peru; I have made some small (but usefull) additions[1] to you (who heard the discourse delivered) may observe, and now for your spiritual use and welfare I commit them to you as the service of your worthy servant in the gospel.

H.A.

A SHORT PREFACE

If aiming for the vain applause of men
From truths like these I must withhold my penn,
O if the frowning world I had to fear
These lines in publick never would appear:
But when my soul inspired with truths so grand,
(Tasting the clusters of the promis'd land.)
And duty calls, I yield to the command.
And O that God may point them to your heart,
That you might feel, and with me share a part!
But if you wish to share the glorious prize
Let no tradition or your will arise,
To vail the scene, and darken both your eyes.
Be bigotry and superstition slain,

44

Then read with earnest cries a pearl to gain;
Like a wise bee search ev'ry field around
Extract where e'er there's sweetness to be found;
For if you would expell the shades of night,
Long as you live stand candidate for light.

* * * * * * * * * *

S E R M O N

*From Mark the 16, 5, And entering into the sepulchre they saw
a young man sitting on the right side, clothed in a long white
garment.* Ecstatic from word 1

CHRIST! O that worthy and transporting name! well
might the Apostle (and let me likewise) say, I am determined
not to know any t[h]ing among you, save Jesus Christ and him
crucified: For his name is not only a strong Tower, but likewise
as ointment poured forth; therefore he is loved, and adored by
virgin souls; yea he is God over all blessed forever more; he is
the theme of angels, and joy of seraphs; he not only replenishes
all heaven with his beauty, but with his smile hath brought
many a mourning soul from the border of despair to Sion's
chambers with songs of joy; yea countless millions from the
Jaws of hell to the realms of everlasting light, with all tears
wiped from their eyes, and their heavy groans turned to shouts
of triumph. O! it was that name (let me say it with reverence
and wonder!) that first taught my wandering soul the long lost
paths of peace, and made me to drink of the long sought for
streams of happiness, and rivers of pleasure, and Ah! It is this
Christ that I expect (when I am lingering on the confines of the
grave) will support and lead me, thro' the dark caverns of death
to the bright abodes of everlasting day, and cause me to sing
when terestial worlds are known no more, and O that he might
be my continual theme while mortal life endures, and wholly
engage my heart and tongue; especially at this time when called
to address this orditary! And ah! I can tell you my hearers it is
with joy of soul, and gladness of heart, that I shall lift both
hand and voice to invite your attention to the glorious theme,
and intreat you to review (with me a few moments) the

45

incarnation, life, labours, sufferings, death, resurrection, conquest, and glory of the world's restorer.

> Attend O mortals, ravished with that name
> Which angels lift on everlasting fame,
> While I with joy will lend my stamm'ring tongue
> To raise a note of that immortal song,
> Till we in heav'n untie the countless throng!

But O methinks my disorders of mind by my fall are so many, my ignorance so great, my darkness so almost impenetrable, and my distance from God so vast, that I am ready to say that (by being so uncapable of doing his name justice), I shall but marr the glorious theme; yet feeling an emulation even with angels, I must attempt the subject, tho' I am but a worm; and O that he who inspired the heart of Jesse's son to speak of his name in the great congregation would release my imprisoned soul and loose my tongue (long clogged with sin) to tell the world that Jesus reigns, and proclaim this day as the disciples when they saw Jehovah riding the rude and unintelligent beast blessed is he that cometh in the name of the Lord! Hosiana in the highest! *(a)* and expecially while at this time I have the happiness of taking a number of young men by the hand, to lead and incourage them on their way to the promised land, instructing them by divine help, for the heavenly war; which will call me to adapt my addresses to those in the bloom of life which altho' may be of benefit to all the young people present, yet designed principle to answer to the request of a number of young men[2] who have collected in this place for the enjoyment and service of God. And O how can I express my unspeakable satisfaction in finding at my return so many in the bloom of life rising up out of the sleep of sin and death, to follow the dispised Nazaune [Nazarene], face a frowning world, and wittness for God before the tents of the ungodly! O may immortal blessing crown your endeavours, and enternal praises thereby be raised to the redeemer's name! ah may you as ornaments of the gospel cheerfully dedicate and wear out the flower of your days in the redeemer's cause, and

(a) Mat. 21, 9

46

allegorical ?

then share in the bloom of immortal youth at Christ's right
hand, where reproaches, storms, death, and sin, is known no
more! But will Jehovah stoop so low as to seat a youth, a
worm, a rebell at his right hand? Yet saith our text they saw a
young man sitting on his right side, signifying at his right hand
which is the grand subject that I am to entertain you with at this
time: And which God grant may be applied to your hearts;
And as I speak for the Lord of hosts, and the welfare of your
souls at stake I dare not spend much time entertaining you with
a dry historical account (as letter preachers is), but shall
indeavour to discover the spiritual sense of our text (together
with some usefull digressions, under four general observations.

First follow the Son of God to the sepulchre, and
examine the nature and spiritual sense thereof.

Secondly the spiritual meaning of this young man being
in the sepulchre.

Thirdly what we are to understand by this young man
being at the right hand of Christ while in the sepulchre.

Fourthly and lastly, what we are to learn of his being
clothed in a long white garment and something of the privileges
of being thus with Christ in the sepulchre. And now as Christ
came down from heaven to our earth and went from the womb
to the sepulchre, according to our first observation, I must take
my hearers by the hand and review the unspeakable sorrows,
hard labours, grand design, agonies, death, and conquest of
this great Messiah while we follow him from the manger to the
sepulchre: And O what surprising and heart-melting scenes
shall be discovered, (omiting his travels and labours during the
four thousand years before he assumed a particular body of
clay) only in the short period of his mortal life! And O has the
grand Visitant appeared; Has the foot of his incarnate love
reached our guilty world, to wade thro' the unspeakable
miseries of our fallen state! Ah! He who thought it no robbery
to be equal with God, took on him the form of a servant. *(b)*
and for what? Why to be come a servant to sinners, and wear
out his life in the service of a miserable rebellious family; yea to
wash their feet, not in water only, but in his own blood.

(b) Phil. 2, 6.

O What a wonder of unbounded grace
Jehovah stoops to save a treacherous race,
Bears all their Pains, and spills his vital blood
To reinstate them in the arms of God.

And how, O how will the sinking world receive him? will they not be ravished and immotral [immortal] raptures to acclamate his bless'd arrival to their (if I may say) starving perishing, and abandoned world? O! no (but must I tell it in Gath or publish it in the secrets of Askelon?) for God declares there was no room for him in the inn (c) and is it so still? Ah there never was nor ever will be any room for him in that heart where the amusing charms, ensnaring joys, and anxious concerns of this world's trading and trafficking have yet the possession; nor yet in the inn of self-righteousness: Witness ye beasts of Bethlehem whose filthy stable, and empty manger first found him room, was not you his first companions? And is it not still with those who not only see and feel themselves as vile as the beasts: but likewise an empty manger, that is whose earthly enjoyments fail them, see the emptiness of all created good like the starving prodigal finds a mighty famine (d) I say it is not with such that he takes up his abode? And rejoice O my soul that with such he deigns to dwell! But to return to his spotless, and yet miserable life, soon we find him, altho' so early in his father's business (e) driven to the wilderness exposed to the inclemency of estimental convultions, the fury of the rude monsters of the wood, the stratagems and wars of the infernal regions without a morsal of bread for the support of his starving and wasting body (f) and then from sorrow to sorrow his trials increasing as he advances in the service, labours and fatigues of the Messiah's office, and soon he has become, (apparently) the off-scouring of all things; the song of the drunkards, a spectacle to God, angels, and men; and naked to all that loss and misery can prey; so that we have already seen him in the sepulchre, a sepulchre indeed, in a spiritual sense, not only abasement, misery and death, but burried, as it were, from all the pleasures, and enjoyments of heaven and

(c) Luke, 2, 7. . (d) Luk. 15, 14. (e) Luk. 2, 49. (f) Matt. 4, 1, 2.

earth. O what an object of pity! And yet as a helpless victim to all the spite, and mallice of earth and hell.

Think, Think, O my hearers! was this for you and me? and yet how often when pinched in some small degree with losses, crosses and disappointments, do you murmur, and think you have a hard lot in the world? When he who gave life and being to all created systems, and with a smile makes arch-angels rejoice in sinking in the depths of misery; a man of continual sorrows, & acquainted with almost insupportable grief. Why if you have not the second garment to your back, or a second meal of victuals for your body, with ever so mean a cottage, to screen you from the storms of this disordered world your earthly entertainments are still far better than his, who was the father of the universe: For foxes have holes, and the birds of the air have nests, but he had not where to lay his head, (g) O then murmur no more at the loss, or want of every thing that this world affords: If you can but live to, walk with, and enjoy the meek and lovely Jesus; for why was his wants and distresses so great, and his abasement so low? Not because he could not have engrossed all the joy, and grandeur of the globe with a turn of his thought: But because his kingdom was not of this world; and consequently its pleasures, and enjoyments were in opposition to his glorious cause; and therefore he partook no more of the enjoyments of this world than was absolutely necessary; and that by no means for the enjoyment of it, or any good, or sweetness he found in it: but wholly for to support him in his state of abasement, (while he was clothed with an elimental body) to endure the hardships of prosecuting his grand design: And yet how many who profess his name, (who have indeed, but the name,) will plead for the indulgence of their earthly joys, pleasures, and recreations: Saying we ought to enjoy this, and may enjoy that for they are given to us for the comforts of life; and there is no harm in wearing this, drinking that, and indulging the other; while others will plead for some, what they call, simple recreations for a relaxation from the burden of an intent mind, but they need not lye. I fear they are not so studious, and will likewise say that we shall

(g) Matt. 8, 20.

bring religion into contempt by being so strict, (tho' little they fear the wounding religion) and fear they shall be guilty of superstition: but O let me tell them not only that such pleas for indulgence is repugnant to the spirit of a true christian, and therefore they are as great strangers to Christ's kingdom as Simon the Sorcerer, but likewise that all such pleas arise from the love of some lust or idol, which if hug[g]ed a little longer may prove their ever-lasting ruin; for he that will save his life shall loose it *(h)* and he that soweth to his flesh shall of the flesh reap corruption: *(i)* for the flesh lusteth against the spirit *(k)* and whatsoever is not of faith is sin, and therefore if there be any such here as I have been pointing out let me intreat you not to deceive your own souls, and like Esau for a morsal of meat sell your birthright, for ye know how that afterward when he would have inherited the blessing he was rejected, and found no place for repentance, altho' he sought it carefully with tears; *(m)* but O for your soul-sake put on self-denial and be willing to lose your life that you may save it, & if you would name the name of Christ make him your pattern, and see not only the self-denial but likewise the unspeakable trials that he went thro'; yea and his disciples likewise; they had as many enemies within as we, and ten thousands more without; they suffered the loss of all their earthly friends, and the esteem of the world, they suffered hunger, thirst, nakedness, and buffeting, in the face (and against the rage) of their innumerable enemies; they were stoned, were sawn asunder, were tempted, were slain with the sword, they wandered about in sheep skins, and goats skins, being destitute, afflicted, tormented, in deserts, mountains, dens, and caves of the earth, *(n)* yea even women were tortered [tortured], suffering cruel mockings, and scourgings, yea more over of bonds and imprisonment not excepting deliverance, when offered, that they might obtain a better, yea and eternal resurrection: *(o)* but I fear you will be wise enough to keep clear of such trials; yea and foollish enough likewise to keep as far from their crown and everlasting reward: unless you make a speedy return. But from my long degression I now return, to follow the lamb of God to the

Stream of Consciousness

(h) Matt. 16, 25. (i) Gal. 6, 8. (k) Gal. 5, 17.
(m) Heb. 12, 17. (n) Heb. 11, 37. (o) Heb. 14, 35.

sepulchre; and O then how small are, or were, all the trials and sorrows of the people of God when compared with the sufferings of their mighty Captain! For if we follow him a little further in his agonizing conflicts we shall find him wading thro' sorrows so unspeakable, and loadened with a weight so innormous as hath diped his vester in blood.

Witness O Gethsemane the cutting pangs, accute tortures and bloody sweat on an almost expiring Jesus? *(p)* and from thence draged, by a band of ruffians, to the cruel bar of injustice, to be sentenced to, and endure all the cruelty that can be invented by all the intestine courts of earth and hell; and O! He dies under far greater miseries and tortures than could ever be inflicted in corporeal punishment by men and devils; neither was their cruelty to his body the cause of his death: But as this will be something new from the common opinion and traditions of men, I must a little enlarge.

And O! Let me intreat my hearers to shake off[f] some of the prejudices of their education, and receive a jewel that may not only be a blessing to your own souls, especially you who are in the prime of life, just coming out to espouse the Redeemer's cause: But likewise arm you against the Arian and Socinian[4] invasions: For their hands have been much strengthened against the truths of the gospel by many preachers and writers, who were labouring to vindicate the gospel, by holding forth that Christ, who was the very God, suffered and died to satisfy God: which the Arians and Socinians say, and well they may from that hypothesis, was God punishing himself to satisfy himself, and fulfil some outward law which man had broken; and thus they say, (using their own comparisons) he takes out of one pocket and puts in the other; which indeed would be evidently inconsistent, as they observe, and yet it is held forth by every one that pretends that Jesus Christ died to satisfy and appease something in God, which they call insensed justice, and vindictive wrath. O! My dear hearers banish, yea forever banish, all such groundless, inconsistent, unscriptural, and God-dishonouring principles, or conceptions, from your mind! For if God hath made some such outward law, the

(p) Luk. 22, 44.

51

breach of which will so insense him, that he must suffer to appease the wrath and repair the injury done to himself, then he hath not only made a law to discover an austere and ostentatious humour, but that exposes himself to an everlasting loss and injury: For, first, if sin could break any such law, as would insense the Deity, then his characture is forever impeached, for the wicked in hell will be forever perpetrating the same crime, and consequently increasing the same injury; to the law and dishonour to his name. Well, but saith one, which I know is the reply of them, that hold forth such an arbitrary insensed God and rigorous law, he will forever punish the wicked in hell for the breach of that law; to which I answer, if I admit your reply, yet you are still as deep in the mire as ever; for you thereby not only dress up a glorious being in rediculous habit, but likewise have fettered yourself with as many inconsistencies as ever; for you have thus not only declared that God is forever punishing the wicked in hell to be revenged, or to receive the penalty, as you say, of that law which they have broken: but likewise that the law must forever remain broken; for every sin deserves as I know you will say, everlasting punishment and as they are continually prepetrating [perpetrating] their crimes to an infinite extreme; so that instead of God being even with them the penalty paid, or the law fullfilled, the breach is infinitely enlarged, the injury increased, and therefore God and his law forever sustaining an increasing loss: for they are forever increasing their rage, sin, and rebellion against him. Besides if Gods justice was insensed, as you say, and his wrath stirred up by so insignificant a being, (in comparison with God) as an angel or man, who may not only stir up his wrath, and insense him: But keep him so forever, then what sort of a God, do you worship? For methinks you must be so well acquainted with the nature of any being insensed or stired up in wrath, as to know that a God insensed, or with wrath stired up in him is not only a God injured and wounded: But a God enraged; and a God thus vexed, injured and enraged, is a God in passion, misery and torment; and a God in torment is a God in hell; O how shocking is the natural constructions of such a principle! And yet I shall be branded by many as an enemy to the gospel, and set as a mark for the arrows of the tradi[ti]onists, because I oppose such principles as holds forth the great Jehovah to be

52

possessed of such a nature, as is the nature of devils. Well saith one, if Christ did not suffer and die to satisfy that Insensed justice, or appease any wrath stired up in God, then what was the cause of all his sufferings? Well my dear hearer, I have been obliged to make a long digression to discover and extract the poison out of your wretched principle: but if you begin now to enquire after light, I shall weary your patience no longer: but with joy pass on to inform you the cause of his sufferings and death, which was what I first proposed; for this his suffering and death, is the sepulchre that he entered in, in a spi[r]itual sense. And first remember that he was not forced to enter this sepulchre: For he declares himself that no man took his life from him; but he laid it down himself freely, *(q)* and therefore they did not force him to any sufferings that was necessary to carry on the redemption; nay God forbid that I should ever attribute any part of my redemption to the cruelty of those blood-thirsty wretches, or imagine that my salvation was in the lest degree depending thereon or carried on thereby; or that it could not be carried on without: for blessed be his name he came down freely for my redemption, and would have completed it if the hands of the ungodly had never touched him; for as for the broken law which he came to fullfill; true it was broken indeed, and he came to fulfill it: But what was that law but the natural reflection of his divine nature; and therefore when man broke off from that God, or turned from the race of life, the law was broke in himself to his own ruin; and now by reason of the contrariety of his nature the reflections of the divine nature (law of the tree of life) became to him as a flaming sword; and therefore the whole work of Christ is to heal the wound, remove the contrariety; thereby fulfill the law for and in the creature, and thereby bring him back, again to a union with and enjoyment of that tree of life in the paradise of God *(r)* and for this end he was obliged to enter in to all the disorders and misery, yea I may say hell, of fallen nature; that is in this fallen and disordered creature to bear (and bring back from) all the contrariety of their hellish nature; labouring with his own incarnate spirit in the fallen creature

(q) John 10, 18. (r) Rev. 2, 7.

untill their contrariety is subdued and will reclaimed and brought back from its state of contrariety to God again; and this labour in the hell of the creatures contrariety was the cause of his suffering, when he saith that his soul was exceeding sorrowful even unto death; (r) and this is the way that God was in Christ reconciling the world unto himself; (s) and declares himself that he suffered that contradiction from the nature of sinners, against himself; (t) and that even to the sheding of blood, which weight of contrariety was the cause of his death, for when he entered in the fallen system at the first instant of man's revolt he became incarnate, for he was then in the flesh (u) and that incarnate spirit was labouring in and under all this contrariety, a sepulchre indeed, untill the period of time that he assumed a particular body of flesh and blood, and then this agony of soul, which before was not visible began to appear, yea so great was his agony of soul, or incarnate spirit in the whole fallen system that when there was no corporeal punishment inflicted on his body, his body, or elemental frame was crushed even to the sheding of blood, under the infinite weight of that contrariety which he was so related to; for you must not imagine that his incarnation was only in that particular body but in, all the fallen system (sentering to that body) the agonies of which forced the blood thro' every pore of his wasting frame (w) and therefore, it is very easy, for you to see that the Jews were so far from being the case of his death, altho' guilty of murder in the strongest terms, that if they had never touched, or laid hands on his body he would, under the infinite weight of that hellish contrariety, labouring in agonies of soul to carry on his grand design, and reclaiming this fallen nature have soon expired and given up the Ghost; that is the agonies of his soul for it was his soul made an offering for sin, being so much greater than his body could bear would have so crushed his body as to overcome and put an end to his mortal life; but at that very instant that he was to expire, for he declares they could not before (v) they had got him nailed to the cross with his arms extended between heaven and earth;

(r) Mark. 14, 34. (s) 2. Cor. 5, 19. (t) Heb. 12, 3.
(u) Rev. 18, 8, 1. Pet. 1, 11._(w) Luk. 22, 14. (v) John 8, 20.

which position of body and manner of dying did import, and discover many important and glorious truths, some of which I will mention.

First, It was between heaven and earth; which was and is still his office as a days man or mediator bringing back from earth (yea from hell) to heaven.

Second, With his Arms extended, good Lord and is thy grace so free that thou not only lived but died with thine Arms extended, stretched to the farthest extend to receive returning Prodigals! Pause a while O my soul! And enter O my hearers, enter the wide leaved gates of eternal felicity display'd by the arms of a bleeding Savoiur! or will some of you at last miss the boundless ocean of everlasting love; surely you are not straitened in Christ but in yourselves (x) fly fly and live forever!

Third, And it was there he give up the Ghost, this proves again my grand assertion that he expired in the agonies of his hard labour, viz. under the weight of fallen nature bringing back the fallen Creature of God.

Fourthly, As Moses lifted up the serpent in the wilderness to heal the poisoned Hebrews, so the Son of Man is lifted up to heal the sin stung souls (y) which likewise discovers to us that salvation is held forth in sight of all the world, as God declares, (z) and thus God holds forth his grace impartially to every one that will except [accept] and be saved thereby. But to return we find from the cross he is taken down, and laid in the sepulchre in the letteral sense, which cannot be denied, but as it was the spiritual sense of our text that I was to discover, I dwelt chiefly on that which I trust you now clearly understand; so that I hope you will never more imagine that he punished himself (for he was God) to satisfy himself, or be at a loss about the cause of his death and suffering, for he suffered even the miseries of hell, (but not as some vainly imagine that after he left the body he went into some other world among the damned, for if he had, he did not tell the thief the truth, for he told him that he should be with him that day in Paradise (g) Yea the greatest part of his life, I may say, he was enduring the anguish and misery of hell, for the absence of God and the

(x) 2 Cor. 6, 12. (y) John 3, 14.
(z) 1 John 2, 2. John 1, 9. Heb. 2, 9. (g) Luk. 23, 43.

weight of sin he endured even unto death, *(a)* which is greatly the miseries of hell. And now if any of my hearers should be at a loss about God's wrath, vengeance, anger, &c (which the scripture so often speaks of) let me inform them two things.

First, That where there is sin and guilt the nature of God is to them as wrath and vengance indeed; by reason of the contrariety which, as before observed, was the cause of Christ's sufferings and agonies, when he had taken so much sin, guilt and contrariety upon himself; and therefore wherever this contrariety remains the nature of God will be as a rock to grind them to powder *(b)*

Secondly, God in infinitive mercy condescends to speak to the fallen creature as things appear to them in their fallen state: but when you are wholly restored back to God you will find he will speak to you plainly without parables *(c)* and likewise find that there is nothing insensed in him: but you had been the wounded insensed and disordered miserable being yourself; and that it was in all these disorders, death and misery that Christ suffered, and all to extricate you therefrom. And Now, let me pause a while or rather, while pointing to the unparellel scene which I have discovered, call on my hearers to exclude the world with every amusing charm of time and sense, and chain the attention of every power of your souls to those grand, those heart-melting, heaven surprising, soul-saving and transporting wonders, and ask, "WAS THIS FOR ME? AND O MY SOUL, WHERE. OF "WHAT, AM I! WHAT HAVE I DONE! WHAT AM I " ABOUT! WHAT MUST I DO! WHERE OUGHT I TO "BE! AND WHERE SHALL I BE FOREVER?

> O love unbounded! love of antient date!
> That brought Jehovah to the dismal ken,
> To drink the dregs of our infernal cup
> Nail'd extramundane to the wood and death!
> O angels gaze to see your maker there!
> And sinners shout, your friend has won the field,
> And in his gore hands you the glorious prize,
> And bids you wear the everlasting Palm!

(a) Mark. 14, 34. (b) Matt. 21, 44. (c) John 16, 44.

56

And O ye sorded souls that are so chained down to the carnal amusements of this wretched world that you cannot give your attention to the glorious scene, nor follow Christ to the sepulchre nor find place in your heart for the suffering God! are you determined still to pass by slite, and reject all the privileges of his dying groans, and rising glory? can you still wag your heads with disdain as you pass by the bleeding Jesus? Will you this day swear for that infernal band that shall commence an eternal war against him and his peacefull kingdom, and utterly abandon yourselves from all the joys of his eternal favour? And after all that has been done choose your portion in that bottomless gulf of fallen nature? Why saith one the man asks a strange question does he think that we are fools, and murderers? It would be strange indeed my dear hearers if it was not true that ye were the worst of fools & murderers: but while you are living in sin and sporting in an unconverted state the broad road to hell it is the most important and consistant question that I can ask you: therefore saith God O ye simple understand wisdom, and ye fools be ye of an understanding heart, *(b)* and I can assure you that a little more sleep, a little more slumber and your poverty, ruin and everlasting destruction will come upon you as an armed man *(c)* and therefore awake ye that sleep, arise from the dead, that Christ might give you life; *(d)* for verily the hour, is coming and now is, that the dead shall hear the voice of the Son of God, and they that hear shall live; *(e)* Jesus the eternal son of God has not only suffered and died, but has this day been so held out to you, that if you still reject, me thinks, I am constrained to say, with Paul, O! Foolish Galatians who hath bewitched you that you should not obey the truth, before whose eyes Jesus Christ hath been this day evidently set forth crucified among you? *(f)* Ah! Well, might he say, you are bewitched, when so seduced by the powers of hell as to disobey the calls and reject the grace of such a bleeding Saviour as hath been discovered to you this day! But time and the greatness of my subject so hurries me, that I must leave you for the present

(b) Pro. 8, 5. (c) Prov. 24, 34. (d) Ephe. 5, 14.
(e) John 5, 25. (f) Gal. 3, 1.

and drop a few more words to the young men for whom I principly designed my Discourse.

And O methinks you that have so cheerfully entered the field for Christ, can but feel renewed obligations and resolutions to fight under the banner of this your mighty Captain, whom you have seen thus spill his blood, and waste his life in the combat with your infernal foes, love him with all your heart, resign life and soul to his name; O call up every power of your souls to follow your glorious conqueror, not only to the crown, but likewise thro' reproaches, trials, and sufferings; or shall I say to the sepulchre, which now brings me to our second observation which was to discover to you the spiritual meaning of the young man being in the sepulchre, where Jesus was and as we have already proved that the sepulchre that Christ went in was his burried state of abasement, sufferings and death, I shall with more ease discover what is now before us; for altho' the young man doth not undergo that misery and sufferings that Christ did, yet he must and does enter the sepulchre with him; for,

First a sepulchre is a place to inter the dead, and those who are born to God and have become members of Christ's body are dead to the enjoyments of this world, and pleasures of time and sense; they are Pelgrims and strangers in the earth, seeking a better country; (g) and therefore their heart and effections are dead to the things of this world, and in pursuit of a life and enjoyment in another; yea, their chief joys are spiritual which this life cannot give them; for God has become their chief good.

Secondly, they are dead unto sin and burried with Christ in baptism, that is Christ spiritual baptism, and then arisen by the power and operation of the same spirit; (h) and thus the sinfull nature of the old man is decreasing and the new man increasing, which burries them more and more from the life and enjoyments of the old; and therefore they may with the apostle say, I die daily, (i) O happy, happy death! I would to God we might all share in this death continually: nor shall we

(g) Heb. 11, 13. (h) Col. 2, 12. 1 Cor. 12, 13. (i) 1 Cor. 15, 3.

ever share in the life in Christ without it; you plead what you will, my dear hearers of your close conformity to externals, or zeal for this and that principle, crying out, when some of your old traditions are crossed, that the cause of Christ is wounded and you must contend earnestly for the faith, I must tell you, you know no more of Christ and his kindgom [kingdom] than your very nature is thus dead unto this world and sin, and make partaker of a new and spiritual life in Christ; and therefore be sure to examine whether you have experienced this death and are longing to be crucified to the world, and have the world wholly crucified to you; and this O YOUNG MEN is the death and new life that I propose to you and would inforce in the strongest terms, and O that Jesus, who harnished [harnessed?] the stripling against the Philistine monster, might arm you with a sling divine, destign and succeed your resolutions, untill you sing the triumphant song with Goliath, the old man that monster of the heart, beneath your feet! then would I repeat the words of God to you and say ye are dead; and your lives are hid with Christ in God; and when Christ who is our life shall appear ye shall also appear with him in glory, *(k)* O go on in your Masters name and strength to attain the glorious conquest! again those who are with Christ in the sepulchre they are not only dead but likewise burried.

First, They are burried by the world, who think it strange saith the Apostle that you run not in the same excess with them, *(l)* yea and the world hates them because they are chosen out of the world, *(m)* they are become a spectacle to the world and a mark for the ungodly; but O fear not little flock for it is your father's good will to give you the kingdom.

Secondly, They are burried from the world by their own choice, for they like Moses had rather suffer afflection with the people of God, than to enjoy the pleasures of sin for a season accounting the reproach of Christ, greater riches than all the treasure of Egypt, *(n)* yea to those two truths, I may call some of this orditary to record, witness ye that have come out from the world to be with Christ, have ye not heard the carnal world saying, that you was under a melancholy gloom, or

(k) Col. 3, 3, 4. (l) 1 Pet. 4, 4. (m) John 15, 1, 9.

strong delusions whereby you have become useless in their jolly company, and are no longer a member of (what they call) civil society, their carnal clubs? And do you not likewise still choose still to be more and more burried from all such carnal company and amusements as once you loved? Yea and God grant that you might be more and more abondant to all the joys and pleasures of this sinfull world!

Ah! Be determined YOUNG MEN (let the world burry you as they will) to make it your chief concern to be with Christ, altho' it may be in a sepuchre; ye be as willing to go with him to Gethsemane as to Olivet, to suffer with him (if called) as to rejoice with him, for you must partake of his sufferings, and be made perfect thro' sufferings, and then O let me tell you that if you suffer with him you shall also be glorified together with him, (p) go on therefore rejoicing that you are counted worthy to bear his reproach, and the God of Jacob be with you. But O let me turn aside to the unhappy part of my hearers who are so in love with the esteem and enjoyments of this miserable world, that they cannot bear to follow Christ in the sepulchre, and be so burried from their carnal joys and company.

O take heed, take heed, my dear friends, lest ye be found like profane Esau who for one morsal of meat (this worlds joys) sold his birth-right (all the privileges of Christ kingdom) and yea know how that afterwards when he would have inherited the blessing he was rejected, and found no place for repentance (no heart to repent) altho' he fought it carefully with tears; that is despairing groans and horible reflections and regret.(o)

How often have you had the spirit of God striving with you, and then you thought you would forsake all and follow Christ: but too soon when you began to think that you must be dispised by your companions Mr. such a one, and Mrs. such a one, would make a laugh at you, & reject you, you returned again to the carnal world and pleasures of Egypt, and so run the risk of loosing the love and favour of God to all eternity, for a few hours of the carnal favour and esteem of those who (if not changed) will e'er long torment you, and be an addition to your misery in hell; but some of you will plead again and say, that

(p) 2 Tim. 2, 12. (o) Heb. 12, 17.

you do not intend to reject Christ, but you love and serve him in private between God and your own soul; which (you say) will be as acceptable with God as if you made so great ado, as some of those that talk so much about religion, and will often make use of those passages of scripture, *if thou have faith, have it to thyself, and cast not thy pearls before swine* &c: but let me tell you that as for that faith you are strangers to it, for the true faith will certainly produce both an inward and outward confermity to God, and a detestation against this carnal world, and God declares that, that faith, which doth not produce good works is dead, *(q)* and as for them pearls you speak of I am sensible that you have none to cast before swine: because those who have them the Lord declares are the salt of the earth, and light of the world, and as cities on hills, *(r)* and your plea is to be private and hid.

O therefore let me intreat you not to deceive yourselves, for the dreadfull moment is at hand, when you will find that to be the word of God likewise, *he that is ashamed of me, and my words him will I be ashamed of before my father, and his holy angels. (s)* The truth is you have some beloved lust or idol too dear to you to be forsaken; and therefore take heed lest God soon say to you as to Ephraim "he is joined to idols, let him alone." *(t)* I have read of a shocking instance of a man and his wife, much of your mind, who lived in a land & day where religion was reviving, and Christ was making up his Jewels, (as I trust he is here now.) and many of their neighbours were convinced and converted, and they began to think that they would likewise want a saviour by and by (a friend in a dying hour) and they agreed to sell their estate and go and join with them people: as it was their custom to have all things common, but they had such a lust for an idol that they had, they concluded to hide it, and when the people made enquiry concerning the idol, they declared before God they had none hid: but God who had been about their private paths, as he is about yours, immediately struck them both dead. *(u)* and we have reason to believe that for the love of that Idol they both went to hell together.

(q) James 2, 17. (r) Matt. 5, 13. 14. (s) Mark 1, 3, 8.
(t) Hos. 4, 17..(u) Acts, 5, 1, 2, 5, 11.

O therefore my dear, dear hearers, take heed that you are not found hiding some wedge of gold or Babilonish garment *(t)* to your everlasting ruin! For thousands and tens of thousands have split upon that dangerous rock; not willing to give up all.

And O let me likewise tell you that if you are ever so happy as to be made partaker of the love of Jesus, and to walk in that way which vulters eyes hath never seen nor the lions welp hath never trode you will not only dispise the joys and esteem of the carnal world: but will count it an honour to bear the cross, and be dispised for Christ sake; and well you may! For then you will have joys that the world can neither give nor take away, and will have Christ to support you: for you will be continually at his right hand which brings me to our third observation:

Which was to discover what is to be understood by this young man being at Christ's right hand while in the sepulchre.

And O lift up your heads ye that are burried with Christ, for although the ungodly world may not only reject you, but follow you with a flood of reproaches: yet Jesus is with you and hears your burdens, for in all their afflictions saith Isaiah he was afflicted and the angel of his presence saved them, *(u)* for you are still tho' in a sepulchre at his right hand.

First his right is engaged for you to deliver you from all condemnation, for there is no condemnation to them that are in Christ Jesus; and therefore let earth rage and hell roar and threaten, yet none shall pluck you out of his right hand, for he will loose none that is there, but raise them all up at the last day, *(v)*

Secondly, His right hand is engaged to fight all your battles, against the powers of darkness and redeem you out of all your disorders; for he will bring you off more than conquerors thro' his everlasting love, and as the mountains are round about Jerusalem so is the Lord round about those that are at his right hand, *(x)* and tho'; the waters sail from the earth, the fig-tree not blossom, the labour of the olive fail, the

(t) Josh. 7, 21. (u) Isa. 63, 9. (v) Rom. 8, 1 John 6, 39.
(x) Sal. 12, 52. [Psal. 125, 2]

fields yield no meat, the flocks cut off from the fold and the herd from the stalls: yet you may rejoice in the Lord, and joy in the God of your salvation; *(y)* and therefore let what will come on the wicked even if there are all swept into hell in a moment all is safe and well with you that are at Christ's right Hand.

Thirdly, The right hand of Christ is engaged not only to give them peace, but the consolations of his holy spirit to support and cheer their souls under all the trials and sorrows of this sepulchred state: and therefore altho' they may have trials and tribulations in the world, yet in him they have peace, ah peace and joy that passeth all understanding, wittness ye happy souls who have sat a moment at his right hand, even when the world was frowning and hell raging, was you not almost constrained to break out with the sweet singer of Israel, surely my lines are fallen to me in pleasant places & I have a goodly heritage, *(a)*

So that while the wicked like the troubled sea are tossed to and fro with ten thousand fears, and exposed to ten thousand dangers, sometimes fearing they shall not attain that degree of the world and its esteem as they are so engaged after, or as others around them; and sometimes fearing that they shall loose what they have; and are jealous that such ones or some of their associates begins not only to get before them, but likewise to treat them with coldness, and disrespect, or even if they do (while present) treat them as their equals, yet they are jealous, it is but disembling, and thus I say, while the wicked are thus tormented with ten thousand distresses and fears to worship and support their miserable and deceitful gods, these at Christ's right hand are setting in peace and drinking large draughts of rest and consolation from that never failing stream ALL THINGS SHALL WORK FOR GOOD TO THEM THAT LOVE GOD, *(b)* and then cheerfull sing,

> Not this small world the kingdom can contain
> Of those that do with Christ in glory reign:
> Then let ten thousand earthly crowns revolve,
> And earth itself with all her joys dissolve,

(y) Heb. 3, 17. (a) Psal. 16, 6. (b) Gen. 28, 16, 17.

We from our throne shall never more be driv'n,
For death itself will but complete our heaven.

And therefore, Fourthly and lastly, When the wicked have wore out their miserable days here, and plunge themselves into eternal perdition, without friend, or helper, joy or comfort, sleep or amusement to mitigate the torments of their despairing souls, those in the sepulchre with Christ will leave their grave cloaths, awake in his likeness and be satisfied with his perfections to sollace in love and reign with him in everlasting glory.

Say O YOUNG MAN does not your heart, begin to burn with love to this lovely name this desire of nations at whose right hand I hope many of you have already sat? Yea, methinks while I am speaking some of you are saying with the antient Bard in his poetry, SURELY THE LORD IS IN THIS PLACE, AND THIS IS NONE OTHER BUT THE HOUSE OF GOD, AND THIS IS THE GATE OF HEAVEN! *(b)* O therefore be incouraged, O YOUNG MAN to go on bearing the reproach of the despised Nazarene without the camp, remembering that he has not only bore the reproaches but infinite sorrows for you; ah! He who is the root and offspring of David, the bright morning star, is your Captain, leader, portion & everlasting joy.

Jesus your Lord will lend you his right hand
To lead and guard you thro' this desert land;
In ev'ry trial stand your bosom friend,
And bear your burdens till your sorrows end.

But I must now lead you to our fourth and last general observation,

Which was to discover the spiritual meaning of this young man being clothed with a long white garment; & O that you may be seen to be thus clothed all your days, and then may your moments glide away with joy.

First, They are internally made partakers of the righteousness of Christ; not imputed as many imagine just, to

(b) Rom. 8, 28.

impartation of X rather than imputation

Antinomian

cover up their sins; or any thing done for them in some distant
region, to answer the penalty of some outward law; and
thereby stand their intercessor at a distance; but the pure spirit
of Jesus Christ in them: for the pure in heart, and they only
shall see God, *(d)* and without holiness no man shall see the
Lord: *(e)* and therefore whoever depends on any
rig[h]teous[ness] of Christ imputed without being, to them,
imparted, will e'er long have cause to take up that bitter
lamentation of the foolish virgins, give us of your oil for our
lamps have gone out. *(f)* For they who are prepared for eternal
glory must really be made to partake of the divine nature here
in this life *(g)* and if any should say that I am denying the
imputation of Christ's righteousness, I answer that I not, only
hold it in the strongest sense: but can easily prove that they are
denying it who hold it in a strict sense any other way: for how
can any thing be imputed to a man and he not make partaker?
Surely if it is imputed it must of consequence be imparted; and
therefore you may take it for a truth of no less importance than
the everlasting concern of your immortal souls, that you will
never be saved by any other imputation of Christ's
rightiousness than the impartation to your miserable sinking
and perishing souls; and thus it is by this impartation of
Christ's righteousness that the young man is cloth in the sight
of God. And thus far as he is made partaker of his divine
nature he is restored to God.

Secondly this divine spirit, and righteousness of Christ
in the heart does naturally produce a cleansing, from sin in the
inward man, and thereby consequently made to forsake and
detest sin in the outward man and therefore brought to a
cheerfull conformity to the ways of God externally, so that
others will thereby behold them clothed in a white garment; as
saith our text, they saw a young man clothed in a white
garment; yea it cannot be otherwise: for where there is fire
there will be light; and therefore, as you have often heard me
declare, a man will no more make me believe that he is a
christian or at Christ's right hand unless I see the white
garment, than he would make me believe that there was a

(d) Matt. 5, 8. (e) Heb. 12, 14. (f) Matt. 25, 8. (g) 2 Pet. 1, 4.

candle burning in my room at midnight when the room is still in midnight darkness: for as certain as God's word is true where there is that immortal principle of light and love in the heart it will give light to the world; *(h)* and therefore saith God if any man be in Christ he is a new creature, old things are done, away and behold all things are become a new; *(i)* and therefore as Joseph, when he made himself known to his brethren changed their raiment, *(k)* so those that have Christ made known savingly to their souls have their garment changed; for they are made partakers of that which does detest every evil, thirst for holiness, and long to be redeemed out of all sin, and to be made pure even as God is pure; *(l)* yea there is no other redemption but to be redeemed out of sin and made like unto God.

And Thirdly this garment of the young man, was not only white but long; and so this divine spirit will finally cleans[e] them throughout, and so transform them that there shall be no spot nor blemish left in them, for saith the Lord it shall be in them as a well of living water springing up unto everlasting life; *(m)* & saith John when he shall appear we shall be like him *(n)* and O let me now enforce this truth on all the proffessors of christianity, especially to you O young men, in the strongest terms remembering that example is far more successful than a bare recept: but by no means would I send you under the thunders of mount Sinai to excite you to the hard task of dressing yourself with the garment of dry obedience without love; but to the flame or immortal love that bled on mount Calvary: one sight of which will constrain you chearfully to put on an external deportment sweetened with the spirit of love to the meek and lovely Jesus, and then the world seeing you clothed with a long white garment will take notice that you have been with Jesus *(o)* and this divine love will not only cast out all fear of death and hell, but cause you to turn a deaf ear to all the flattering charms of this ensnaring world; and likewise set your face as a flint against all its frowns, yea and cause you to take cold death by the hand without reluctance, and defy the terrors of an approaching grave; and

(h) Matt. 5, 14. 2 Cor. 6, 17. (k) Gen. 45, 22.
(l) 1 John 3, 3. (m) Job. 4, 14. (n) 11 Job. 3, 2. [1 John, 3, 2.]
(o) Acts 4, 13.

this will lay the welfare of your poor fellow men so near you[r] heart as to cause you at every opportunity to warn them with tears to fly from the wrath to come, point the wounded to the bleeding wounds of you[r] all-conquering Captain, and court them to the unspeakable joys of his kingdom: that they might enlist under the same banner, fight in the same heavenly war, and share with you in the glorious spoil, when your master shall have won the field, attained the victory and given you the glorious prize to enjoy; at thought of which methinks your hearts begin to burn; O the thoughts of availing, (if I may say) to that vast angelic continent, where wars never wage, foes never come, crowns and kingdoms never revolve, nor laws never change; O the glory of such immortal scenes! How doth the divine attraction call up every power of you[r] transported souls while I speak and cause you to thirst, long, resolve, and re-resolve for CHRIST AND HIM ONLY! Yea methinks, some carnal youth that has long set at nought the friendly warnings of heaven, and turned a deaf ear to the voice of the lovely charmer, that has charmed so wisely, begins to feel some consultations in their breasts and say with Agrippa *thou almost perswadest me to be a christian* and if so, O for your soul sake do not like him put it of[f] for an uncertain hereafter, for I can assure you, you will never have a more convenient season than the present moment besides if you was sure like the expiring thief as I supose you often promise yourself, to find mercy in the last moment! you would not only loose all the prime of life but likewise wade thro' one continual scene of sorrow and uneasiness: for I can tell you by woefull experience the danger, inconsistancy and misery of seeking happiness in this vain world! Upward of twenty years[5] I rejected the waiting Saviour and sought happiness in created good, where it never was nor never will be found and had the nature of a christian too, but then thro' boundless grace I adhered to the voice of the heavenly lover and cast my naked and perishing soul at his feet, O! I found that that kingdoms nor worlds could not parallel! Peace, and joys divine; yea joys unspeakable & full of glory; Ah it was then I drank with ravishing delight from those river of everlasting consolation that makes glad the City of God; Ah that wine that cheers the heart of God and man! *(p)* yea and

(p) Judg. 9, 13.

since the first moment that I knew the joyfull sound I can say Lord ever more give me this joy and living water for I can say with the poet, to set one day beneath thine eye.

> And hear thy gracious voice
> Exceeds a whole eternity
> Employ'd in carnal joys.

Ah did you but know, my dear young friends, the happy moments we often enjoy when sitting, altho' here in the sepulchre, at the right hand of king Jesus, you would not only envy us: but break thro' all opposition and say with Ruth intreat me not to leave thee or to return from following after thee for whether thou goest I will go, and where thou lodgest I will lodge, thy people shall be my people, and thy God my God; where thou diest will I die, and there will I be burried: the Lord do so to me and more also' if ought by death part thee and me *(q)* there are many of us here I trust bound by the grace of God to see the promised land and can say the same; and O let me tell you that we should rejoice in your company, take you by the hand, to run the christian race; O give your hearts to Jesus, join the sacred bond, and go arm in arm with us to the glorious mansions prepared by your Captain for all his dispised followers. Methinks I hear some saying again if all this be true, *which* ALLINE *declares, why should I not be prevailed with? why should I loose such unspeakable joys & destroy my soul forever for the empty sound of a few hours amusement? Methinks I will resolve a speedy escape, but O will God assist me, and have mercy on one so vile?*

Yea my dear friends so ready is God to help, that all heaven will be engaged on your behalf to espouse your everlasting welfare, Saints pray for you, mercy calls you, heaven invites you, and angels wait to raise a note of joy at your return; and O above all! God himself stands with extended arms inviting you to the bosom of eternal joy.

Ah methinks I hear the waiting Father saying, with joy, "MY LONG DESERTING SON BEGINS TO BE IN WANT, AND IS RESOLVING A RETURN FOR BREAD, AND

(q) Ruth 1, 16, 17.

GLADLY WILL I MEET HIM: YEA, LEST HE BE DISCHARGED, I WILL RUN TO MEET HIM, TO HASTEN AND ENCOURAGE HIS LINGERING RETURN." *(r)* O sinner, and what would you more? The fatted calf is killed, the best robe is prepared, and a ring for your finger, yea all things is ready come, O come to the marriage.

> Forsake the world dispise the empty joy,
> Act like a hero, life and soul employ
> To gain the field, and win immortal joy.

But time hurries me I must turn to the young man in the sepulchre, and conclude my message for to you O men I call, and my voice is to the sons of men, and especially to you that late profess Jehovah's name; and O I trust have known his love! and if so go on ye heavenly warriors cheerfully to spend and be sent for your masters cause, and the honour of his great name I speak unto you, as saith John, YOUNG MEN because ye are strong, and the word or God abideth in you and ye have over come the wicked one *(s)* Ah happy YOUNG MEN thus to get the victory over the powers of darkness in your bloom of life before so married to your fallen state that you cannot come and chained down to final impenitance! and O remember that Jesus who has wore out his life for you in a field of blood is still at hand with an immediate & full supply for all your wants as long as you tread this mortal stage! and soon, Ah! soon will call you from your mortal watch to the mansions of eternal glory!

And therefore O let me again and again intreat you to turn every stone, and concert every method for the advancing of his glorious kingdom in your own souls and others during the short period of your mortal stay.

Remember that immortal souls are invaluably precious, and O should you be the means of reclaiming one from eternal misery to the knowled[ge], of Christ, it would be ten thousand times more to you than the gaining of both Indias.

(r) Luk. 15, 20. (s) 1 John 2, 14.

But O instead of that if some of you by growing cold and dead, should get involved in the carnal pleasures and amusing charms of this vain world how would you thereby bring up an evil report against the good land, and perhaps unhappily prove the means of some soul's eternal ruin!

But God forbid, that one of you should be of them that draw back to perdition! And let me now use the freedom to drop one word of advice respecting your manner of publick worship; and here altho' I doubt not but you meant for the glory of god in having your meetings something private, because you I imagined that the scoffing world would make a mock at your small gifts and graces, & broken improvements, yet I can but intreat you to come out boldly for Christ, and not only improve all the gifts of prayer and exhortation that is among you, which by improving will increase, but likewise open the door for (yea invite) the attendance of both saints and sinners; for allowing than many around you are the greatest scoffers and nay even come with a design to make a mock at religion: yet if they would mock there they would else where; and further I must tell you, I know of no way so likely to reclaim them from their mockery as to hold up the light before them, and draw them with the cords of love; and further I would observe (not by way of reflection) that some of you who are now rejoicing in the God of your salvation, I have reason to suppose was once in the same darkness with them, but the gospel being openly proclaimed, and hearing so much of Christ and the privileges of his kingdom, you was thereby constrained to embrace the Christ and espouse the cause you once despised and rejected; besides you cannot be bound too strong to be wholly for Christ, and therefore, your coming out publickly to witness for his name may be a bulwark around you against strong temptations, and for my part I would not desire any back door open to the world for me to step out and commit sin, saying *I never professed to be a Christian.* But I think it a privilege to profess, and that publicky, therefore be not afraid any of you, of being under too great obligations, or being too much watched by both saints and sinners. I should not have said so much, but fearing that some of you may too much indulge the fear of man, and thereby fall into a cold dead state: and O if I should, in the course of providence, once more tread this part of the vineyard, how much more would the melancholy news of your desertion (even one of you) from the cause of Christ pierce my soul and wound my heart than the solemn toll of your passage thro' the grave!

O therefore let me again and again reinforce my earnest intreaties for your perseverence in a close walk with God; and then when I am treading the different parts of the globe, wading thro' the storms and reproaches of an ungodly world and the trials of an unsanctified heart to blow the jubilee trump; the Hebrews release; and with the glad news of our maker's name to the gentile world, hear O hear me and my labours continually on your mind in your wrestling cries to the throne of grace; and O I trust when distant mountains with their towering summits, or the wrestless ocean with her bellowing waves far part our distant Bodies that our minds shall be one cemented in that indissolvable band of everlasting love; and often meeting in our joint cries to heaven; and O, if not before, when a few more hours of grief and labour have run their speedy rounds I trust thro' the boundless grace of him that has loved us we shall quit the ten thousand disorders of our fallen state, awake, and meet out of the sepulchre, but still by Christ's right hand with the countless band of adorers to sollace in his immortal love; where foes never invade, storms never beat, parting hours, sin, death and interposing clouds are known no more; and O shall I say there to be one with this our lovely Jésus, and join thro' all the realms of eternal felicity in one harmonious strain of praise to his worthy name: which God of his infinite mercy grant, AMEN.

THE YOUNG MAN's SONG[6]

I.

WE from Egypt's slavish Ground.
On our Way to Canaan bound,
As we journey with us sing
A loud Anthem to our King.

II.

We superior do esteem
The Reproach of JESUS Name.
Than in Egypt's Treasure roll'd,
Or, Sons of Pharaoh's Daughter call'd.

III.

Earthly Lovers we'll adieu;
JESUS Love, and him persue;
All Reproaches disregard:
Nor will think our Trials hard.

VI.

CHRIST before us bore our shame;
Hell blasphemed his spotless Name;
All that will this CHRIST persue.
Share in his Reproaches too.

V.

Let us then go boldly on,
Fix our Eyes upon the Crown;
Soon in Glory we shall rise
To enjoy the lasting Prize.

VI.

Come poor Sinners share a Part.
Give this blessed CHRIST your Heart,
We will take you by the Hand;
Go with us to Canan's Land.

VII.

Leave your carnal Loves and Toys;
Share with us in sollid Joys,
Let the world your Names disdain
You shall soon in Glory reign.

VIII.

But if JESUS you dispise,
For a Shaddow lose the Prize,
We shall bid you all adiew;
By his help we'll him persue.

IX.

If with us you will not go,
Nor the love of JESUS know,
Soon you must awake in Hell:
While in Glory we shall dwell.

X.

Soon our hav'nly Friend will come
To receive his Pilgrims home;
Hark! ye Pilgrims hear him say
"Come ye Mourners come away.

XI.

Then we'll join the countless throng,
HALLILUJAH'S all our Song;
Where with Wonder we shall see
Him that dy'd for you and me.

XII.

Hark! "AMEN" the Angels sing,
HALLILUJAH to your KING"!
Hail, ye happy Pilgrims then!
Ev'ry Tongue shall say AMEN.[7]

NOTES:

1. It would be interesting indeed to know precisely what these "additions" were and how Alline actually transformed the spoken word into a printed pamphlet. It is known that Alline wrote a form of shorthand and it may have been that his published sermons were based upon three previously prepared shorthand versions. On the other hand, one of his Liverpool disciples might have copied into shorthand Alline's three sermons and then transcribed them for the Falmouth evangelist who then edited them. What is certain, however, is that the printed sermons faithfully reflected what Alline actually preached in the Liverpool region in 1782 and 1783.

2. Often in his preaching, Alline would focus on one specific group in his congregation and then another. This proved to be a very effective technique.

3. Alline was very explicit about the special "spiritual" way in which he interpreted the scriptures.

4. "Arian and Socinian" were Alline's codewords for Unitarian. He was very concerned about the growing strength of the Unitarian movement.

5. From a detailed description of Alline's conversion see Beverley and Moody, *The Journal of Henry Alline*, pp. 29-66. Alline first experienced the "moving" of "the spirit of God" when he was "about eight years of age," in 1755 or 1756. (*Ibid.*, p. 29).

6. This hymn was enthusiastically sung by Alline's followers in the 1790's. See, for example, Harris Harding to Judah and Mrs. Wells, August 25, 1791, in G.A. Rawlyk (ed.), *New Light Letters and Songs* (Hantsport, 1983), p. 138.

7. It is noteworthy that the title page of the copy of Alline's November 19, 1782 sermon, deposited in the Archives of Acadia University, contains the following handwritten inscription:

to her by her friends in Liverpool
May God inspier hir heart with Grase
wha ere she look
that She may Walk in Ways of Life
and flee from Every Sin
Mary Lock Apr. 20, 1788

I have not been able to find any biographical information
about Mary Lock. She obviously was one of Alline's most
ardent disciples.

A
SERMON
On a Day of THANKSGIVING
PREACHED at LIVERPOOL,

By HENRY ALLINE.

on the 21st, of November 1782.

* * * * * * * * * *

HALIFAX. Printed by A. HENRY

Shows attitude of "Yankee Neutrals" toward Rev.

THE PREFACE

REQUESTED by a number of my Friends, (who I trust were laiming at the Glory of God and good of Souls) I with cheerfu[ll]ness commit this to the Publick; And O may Jesus my Blessed Master not only pour a Hundred fold Reward into their Bosom: but likewise spread it's usefulness to Thousands of their fellow men, yea to generations yet unborn, and thereby bring immortal Honours to his Name!

May he whose love call'd forth the Angellic Train,
To sing with Joy thro' Heav'ns immortal plan,
And from the blaze of uncreated day
Has deign'd to bleed in cloths of sin and clay
That he might his own boundless love display
Hand this abroad by his own sacred Dove,
To teach immortal souls redeeming Love!
Read meek enquirer with a thirst divine,
I'll be thy waiter and the blessing thine;
And while you read my Heav'ns own balmy wing
Awake with Joy the deathless mind to sing
'A theme like this MY JESUS IS MY KING,
'AND GREAT THY LOVE, HOW BRIGHT THY
   GLORIES SHINE,
'FROM THY OWN WOMB DISPLAY'D SUCH
   FLOODS DIVINE
'TO MAKE THYSELF AND ALL THY GLORIES
   MINE!
FAIN WOULD I SING THE MERITS OF THAT
   BLOOD
I SEE THE WOUNDS! AWAY CREATED GOOD!
MY HEART AWAKES MY JESUS IS MY GOD.
AND STILL DESCEND O THOU IMMORTAL
   DOVE
ATTRACT MY PANTI[N]G SOUL TO REALMS
   ABOVE,
AND WRAP ME IN THE MANTLE OF THY LOVE.
THERE WHERE THY GLORIES IN MERIDIAN
   BLAZE
MY RAVISH'D SOUL WOULD EVER ON THEE
   GAZE,

AND HUMBLE ANTHEMS TO JEHOVAH RAISE:
AH THIS WITH ALL THE UNIVERSAL THRONG
SHALL BE MY JOY, MY GLORY, AND MY SONG,
JESUS MY ALL! TO HIM BOTH PRAISE
BELONG.

* * * * * * * * *

Occasional T-Giving

S E R M O N

From Psalm 107, 31. Oh' that Men would Praise the Lord for his Goodness, and for his Wonderfull works to the Children of Men.

METHINKS in some degree with the Prophet of old I can say I was glad when they said unto me, let us go up into the House of the Lord; our feet shall stand within thy Gates O Jerusalem, whether the Tribes go up, the Tribes of the Lord, unto the testimony of Israel to give thanks unto the Name of the Lord *(a)* for I not only with Joy embrace the privilege, for the Joy of my own Soul but am happy likewise to find such a General Attendance, and am thankfull to find the heads of Families, and leading Men of the place have so generally answered my last Sabbaths request,[1] to exclude their secular employ, and have used their influence for the same on others under their charge; and O I would hope you have not only given your Attendance but that with ardent disires for grace to make this a day of thanksgiving indeed.

And O that he who inspired the fisherman at Penticost would cause a sound from heaven as of a mighty rushing wind to shake the Earth, alarm the hearts of this auditory and loose my Tonge (long cloged with sin) cloven the Truths I deliver with his spirit as a divine interpreter, open and apply them to every heart, and as your various wants may require, that the blind might see, the deaf hear, the dead rise, the lame leap for Joy, and the dumb speak forth the praises of his worthy Name,

(a) Psa. 122, 3.

79

and that all our hearts as one warmed with his love, and a feeling sense of his unchangable kindness might with cheerfullness of soul praise him for his goodness and for his wonderful works to the children of men!

And if this be your expectation or desire, O let me intreat you one and all to exclude the world with all its amusing charms, and say to the Earth with all its allurments even the most warrentable concerns of life, to every wandering thought, to every slavish fear, and to all supinity as Abraham to his young men *(b)* TARRY YE HERE WHILE I GO AND WORSHIP YONDER; then may you expect Jesus to meet and supply your innumerable wants, cheer your souls with his smiles, and cause you to say with his disciples at Olivet IT IS GOOD FOR US TO BE HERE *(c)* and then may you return to your houses and visit your bed-chambers with joy rejoicing in, and telling of what the Lord had done for your souls.

And Oh! how would my soul rejoice, when thro' being in the least degree instrumental for your good, I could return bearing my sheaves with joy! And it is the goodness of God leads sinners to repentance, and the love of Christ constraineth us to love him, I shall endeavour (being obliged likewise by the subject now before us, and design of the day) to point you to God's unspeakable goodness, or lead you to the fountain of his unbounded love, that you may thirst after, drink of, and be ravished with, the glories, love, and goodness of Jehovah, so as to break out in raptures of joy with the Prophet, and say, "O that men would praise the Lord for his goodness and his wonderful works to the children of men!"

And as our Text is rather a note of surprise, and a grateful acknowledgement annexed to, and extorted by the preceeding view of the infinite goodness, love and compassion of God, I shall be obliged to have continual recourse to the preceeding subject to discover that goodness which seems to have extorted the prayer, the praise and the joyful surprise, together with desires insatiate, that God might be loved and adored by the sons of men. Nor do I know of any thing that would so make this a day of thanksgiving, cause your hearts to

(b) Gen. 22, 5. (c) Luk. 9, 33.

burn with love and glow with gratitude, as this grand subject, the goodness of God, and his wonderful works to the children of men, if discovered and applied to your hearts by the spirit of God; which subject I shall endeavour (for to ease your attention and assist your understanding) to exhibit under three general observations, together with some useful digressions.

1st. I shall discover something of this goodness in itself.

2dly. The communications of this goodness breaking forth in creation.

3dly. In Redemption.

4thly. In the preservation of the fallen system for Redemption.

5thly. The instances of his goodness to us in particular: all of which expresses the goodness of God and his wonderful works to the children of men; & as I shall endeavour to improve the same by making an application, I shall, singularize my hearers as in their degrees and several stations of life; and O! for an earnest groan from every heart that Jesus, who teaches as never man taught, would descend and reside over this assembly with the dews of immortal love, to water, soften, and cheer every heart with the wonders of redeeming love!

And now to return to our first general observation I am to discover to you something of this source of all goodness, and cause of every communication of love: And here, altho' my sentiments may be singular yet true, and attracting to all those who stand open to conviction; for notwithstanding the greater part of our expositors of divine revelation hold forth the work of creation, redemption, and every expression of mercy to the sons of men, to be a strained stoop, and singular act of his kindness, yet I believe, and can easily prove that it is not only a free act of love, but likewise the natural product of that infinite over-flowing, yea, I was about to say, uncontainable goodness; that is that God in himself is possessed of, yea his very nature is such as not only to love goodness, but delight to do good; and let others say or pretend what they will of their loving God and admiring his divine perfections, I dare not act the hypocrite or dissemble with God; for I know it would not be possible for me to love such a God and admire the nature of such a Being that did all the good he did, not as a free and natural act, but only a strained and singular expression of pity and kindness and that in partiallity too, shewing favour to me and leaving a number of my poor family to perish, when their misery was no benefit to him and he could be as kind to them all if he would, and save them all too but would not; I say I am far from believing it possible for me (unless I am kept in blindness) to love and admire such a being with a voluntary will, and cheerfulness of soul; but when I am blessed with but a glimmering ray of the truth, and see God as he really is in himself possessed of that Goodness that takes delight in doing good, yea so self necessary and unboundedly good that he can neither act partially nor withold his goodness from every vessel that can receive it, or creature that desires it, (c) yea this self existent fountain of goodness wisdom, glory and beauty, is the joy and happiness of God himself, and that wine that cheers the heart of God and Man, (d) and this fountain of goodness is the joy of all the angelic hosts; this is the joy of my soul now, and I trust my ravishing delight to all eternity: and this fountain of unbounded goodness is the moving cause of every communication of love to his creatures; yea and the very cause of creation: O then what goodness! what infinite goodness! ah! soul ravishing goodness is this! surely I may break out with acclamations of joy and surprise with the Prophet, "O that men would praise the Lord for his goodness and for his wonderful works to the children of men! for he is infinitely good, yea he is altogether lovely!" (e) And say my dear hearers, does not this discovery of the glorious scene attract your whole souls, or kindle a spark of immortal glowing and unextinguishable love for such a God? O love him; love him my fellow mortals, love him with all your souls, surely he is worthy of all your love; yea how can you but love him, when he is love, even the perfection of love itself! it's true you have cause to rejoice in redemption from eternal misery; but he is but a mercenary christian who is possessed of no higher love than that; yea I am almost ashamed to invite you to heaven, because there is a hell; but because there is a God in heaven; yea a God, that is heaven itself.

(c) Psa. 145, 16. (d) Num. 9, 13. (e) 1 John 4, 8.

For Oh! a God of boundless love like this,
Is an unbounded sea of perfect bliss!
Dive, dive, my hearers th' unfathomable sea,
There's room for souls as vile as you and me!

But to return and drop a few more words on my intended subject, and that is, that such is the self-existence and infinite fullness of this goodness as it cannot possibly receive any injury or benefit, nor can possibly be glorified by receiving but only by giving, and whatever is done by this goodness is by no means to add to the glory, or bring something to the goodness and grandeur, but wholly to display that love and manifest that goodness which was already existing in God, and thereby not to receive happiness or glory, but to display happiness and glory; and yet, Oh! too shocking to mention! how is it held up in a land of light, that God, for his own glory, has designed, or consented to the everlasting damnation of countless millions of his creatures; but as I trust God is about to expell that hellish darkness from the poor blinded world, and has already delivered most of his people in this part of the vineyard from them disagreeable chains, I shall return and say, *God will have mercy and not sacrifice;* — but what did I say! will have mercy and not sacrifice! O sinners! sinners! hear the glorious news; for you are not only indulged with the glorious news, but commanded to believe, receive and rejoice in the infalible, and soul-transporting truth; *go ye,* saith my master, *and learn what that meanth,* — *I will have mercy and not sacrifice.* (e) Oh! that men would praise the Lord for his goodness, & for his wonderful works to the children of men! And now I am come to our second observation, which was to discover something of the communications of this unbounded goodness in the work of creation; and this I shall be able to discover in a few words, for as we have found God to be such a self-good being, as to be excluded from any possibility of receiving benefit or injury and all his divine opperations of love and goodness are the natural product of that infinite fountain of love and goodness, then consequently the cause and design

(e) Matt. 9, 13.

of all creation must be to manifest and display the overflowing goodness and infinite love of such a being or to adapt my discourse to the weekest capacity of my hearers, let me say made Vessels to fill with love, that is hungry creatures to feast upon his goodness, receive his grace, enjoy his love and be forever happy in his Transporting perfections and that from himself, and of his own goodness, and in his own likeness, he brought forth an innumerable crowd of immortal beings forever to partake of their Father's love and goodness and sollace in the unbounded Sea of his self-existant perfections.

Think O think my dear hearers, ye fallen offspring of such a being, what a Father you once had! it was not possible for him to have any motive in view but the display of his glory the manifesting of his love infinite love, and the making you eternally and unspeakably happy in the enjoyment of it. And altho' so many in the world have held the reverse yet if you only admit that creation was moved for any thing else, or that God for his own glory even consented to the misery and eternal damnation of his creatures, the natural consequences are so obviously infamous that we should dress a glorious being in a ridiculous habit, nor could I ask you to love and adore such a God, who consigned or left the greatest part of his creatures to the inexpressable Torters [Tortures] of eternal despair, when he might have saved then without any injury to himself. But saith one if God be a God of such overflowing goodness, why are so many at last (as even yourself say) eternally miserable? To which I answer (as many of you have often heard me) because they reject that redeeming hand until they are sealed down in that hardness and final impenitency that the spirit of God (which is in itself much meekness and humility as cannot force itself against the creatures will) can have no effect on them; yea the more it strives with them after that, the lower it sinks them from redemption or he would labour with them more. (f) and God declares himself that he not only would have brought them to the enjoyment of his love but has often laboured with them for that end: but they would not be redeemed, (g) and therefore he saith ye will not come unto me that ye might have life (h) so that altho' God's love is infinite,

(f) Isa. 1. (g) Luk. 16, 34. (h) John 5, 40.

his goodness overflowing and he takes delight to make his creatures happy therein, yet if you harden your hearts against it, it can be of no more benefit to your souls than the light of the sun to a blind man.

O therefore let me intreat you for your soul-sake if ever you expect to be made a partaker of God's infinite goodness, and drink of the boundless Ocean of his love do not by rejecting the spirit of Jesus seal yourselves within yourselves to impenitrable darkness, and thereby sink in your own regions of eternal despair beyond the reach of infinite love and goodness: For the hellish and malicious contrariety of your fallen nature will soon, not only seal you down beyond the reach of mercy, but forever rage against that mercy yea and the love and goodness of God will be so contrary to you that it will forever infinitely augment your mesery and add to the Torters [Tortures] of your keen despair: but if now in time while you are held up for that end you adhear to the redeeming spirit of God get your will turned, your hellish contrariety removed, and you transformed to the likeness and purity, of God you will for ever find to your unspeakable Joy that this God is as I tell you, yea Ten Thousand times more so, nothing but love and goodness in all his divine perfections; and you will see clearly that he was so infinitely happy and independantly glorious that he was so far from expecting any addition either by your happiness or misery that it was for the display of his goodness and manifesting of his love that he brought forth, all creation and that he was possessed of such Goodness that this great expression of his love was but a natural manifestation of himself; or the natural production of his own perfections. O then it is no wonder that we hear David breaking forth in this joyfull surprise and impatient desire O THAT MEN WOULD PRAISE THE LORD FOR HIS GOODNESS! But it is a greater wonder (tho' lamentable) that all the Sons and Daughters of Men are not raptured with the same truth, and engaged in the same Notes. And O methinks I am constrained to lift my Heart, my hand, and my voice, and in the Name of God, and in the presence of this Assembly, and declare, that GOD IS LOVE and make use of the most forceable arguments and endearing intreaties to devose [divorce] your minds from every other lover, and espouse you to this Husband, wean you from all created good, and lead you to those Rivers of

85

uncreated good, and seas of pleasure, that thy God, thy creator, thy preserver, thy redeemer, thy life, thy joy, and everlasting reward is possessed of.

But O can I think, and must I believe, that the greatest part of mankind, yea even of this Society are so involved in ignorance, so abandon to reason, and so infatuated by the powers of Hell, and regions of darkness, that they will refuse reject and dispise such ravishing, delights, such sollid good, lasting pleasures; and unparelled Grandure, while indifatiguably in persuit of shaddows, wearing out their lives for an empty sound, eating husks with the Swine, and licking of dust with the Serpent, untill in a moment they are in the agonizing confusions of an irreparable loss and plundged in despair for ever to rue the folly of their miserable cruelty and irricoverable deception where hope can never come! good God awake the world, and save them from the infernal attraction of those wandering stars, and lead them, O thou bright and morning star to the fountain of life before their fatal dye is unalterably cast; and awake, O my hearers, from the dangerous amusements of this ensnaring World, for it is a stage of snares, a theatre for murder; O therefore awake and no longer squander away your few fleeting moments sporting on the confines of eternal perdition.

O think a moment what you was made for and what a capacious and immortal soul you are endowed with and risk it no longer in the Jaws of Hell: for it is now a market day and immortal Crowns are to be attained without money and without price.

Yea this very day Jesus is proposing his blood to cleanse you, his grace to forgive you, his spirit to lead you, himself for your friend husband and Father, and his love to cheer you, and all his divine perfections to make you everlastingly happy and glorious. O that I could allure you with his charms, court you with his smiles, and draw you with the cords of his love to begin your thanksgiving and receive your mansion in the realms of unchangeable felicity!

I now return to our third observation, which was to discover the communcations of this goodness in redemption. And O what shall I say of love so infinite and goodness so unbounded! and how can I speak of the unparallel condescention, and my heart not melt! Had he have turned a thought of Love and sent an Embassy of Peace by some ministring Cherub I should have cause forever to love wonder and adore.

But O how much more when he himself is the Ambassador, and wears out his life in the grand Errand! Ah and the act of grace to rebells too! O what shall I say! Or how express the Truth so infinitely Glorious! Angels will foreever acknowledge themselves lost in the unfathomable Ocean, and confess their utter inability of Telling the greatness of that love and goodness, which to their surprise stooped for the redemption of our miserable and rebellious System, at the infinite expence of suffering and death.

And O could it be! was his goodness so unbounded and his love so uncontainable! Ah it is a Truth; and equally as true that it was not a strained act, or scanty expression of kindness but free and liberal, and of choice, an act of goodness like himself; naturally consistant with the greatness of his love and goodness.

And now think my dear hearers what love what infinite love he is possessed of; surely you will be convinced that his nature is all love self-existant and overflowing goodness; behold he comes freely yea of choice without any intreaties from the needy and with an act of grace for the life and salvation of his enemies, when he knew it wonld cost him infinite sorrow, in the agonies of death view him in the manger in that state of abasement even among the beasts sinners behold thy redeemer; and angels behold thy God an infant of a span long cast out from the Society of Angels, and men, to endure the rage of earth and hell, view him sweating in Gethsemane in accute torters [tortures], and unsupportable agonies of death under your enermous guilt till blood is forced from every pore, beneath the crushing mountain; and ask O ye Sons and Daughters of Adam WHY WAS ALL THIS? And let your hearts break for sin while melting with love, and surely you will Break out in the language of our Text.

O THAT MEN WOULD PRAISE THE LORD FOR HIS GOODNESS, AND HIS WONDERFULL WORKS TO THE CHILDREN OF MEN! Or are you so chained down to impenitrable hardness and insensibility, as never to hear or feel those groans which if possible would have made arch Angels tremble, *O my Father if it is possible this cup may pass away nevertheless, if man can be saved no other way, not my will but thy will be done?*

And is it possible for you to spend day after day, year after year, lye down and raise, go out and come in with your sorded minds so chained to the beggarly amusements, empty toys, and mercenary pleasures of this base stage as never to find room in your debauched Hearts for Truths so grand, and, to you, so important? O leave your little world, your contracted orb, your polluted Ken, and Soar to the realms of Angellic delight, give your poor imprisoned minds aloose but a moment in search of worlds yet to you unknown; court immortal Loves, and drink of those Rivers of [p]leasure that makes glad the City of God, and taste those joys of ancient and neverfailing date.

Surely you have been long enough slaves to sin and Vassals to satan Methinks you must by this time begin to groan under the Yoke of Pharaoh in the bondage of Egypt, aud be willing to ventur out for the promis'd land. And O let me tell you that Jehovah is come down burning with love and the Bush is not consumed. *(i)*

Ah Jesus has not only spread the mantle of his love over the lost world in general, but over you in particular; for your villages and Families happly enjoy the droping of the sanctuary and effusions of his holy spirit. Oh hear his calls, receive his grace, enjoy his love, and adore his Name for his goodness to the Sons of Men.

But to return to the infinite expence of the display of this goodness, we find this meek and lovely Jesus after standing as a mark for the ungodly, and enduring all the reproaches of men, and rage of hell, thro' the whole period of his meserable life, he is crushed under the weight of fallen nature and expires in the agonies of insupportable anguish and misery. Ah well might the earth tremble, the rocks rend the graves open, and the meridian sun wrap his face in a melancholly shroud, when Jehovah himself was enveloped in darkness, and struggling in the pangs of death and miseries of Hell.

(i) Exo. 3, 2.

And is my God nail'd to the fatal Tree?
Good God and are those cuting pangs for me!
O melt my heart! my senseless soul arise,
And fountains flow from both my wishfull eyes.
Then soar my soul in greatfull songs of love,
To reach thy Jesus in the realms above.[2]

But O a lamentable sound has stole my attention from the glorious scene! What is that says you, why the careless unaffected and rejecting world crying out while passing by with wagging heads *crucify him, crucify him:* and you ah you ye careless souls who are wasting your days in vanity are the cruel and unhappy beings: for if you have not fallen in love with him, and received him in your hearts as your chief good leaving every other lover for his sake ye are still among his enemies and your conduct cries out *away with this fellow and release unto us Ba[r]abbas* for you are sparing and hugging your sins your lusts and Idols those thieves and murderers: Ah those murderers of Christ and of immortal souls yea and not only the careless and profane world are guilty of this crime but likewise you that have the Name and form of godliness but are enemies to the spirit and power; for the high priests Scribes and Pharisees could very zealously cry out the Temple of the Lord the Temple of the Lord, and at the same time with all the malice of Hell stop and crucify the Lord of the Temple.

O return from your sin, your cruelty, and folly, not only ye careless and profane, but ye dry formalists ye Christless christians: or if I may say with the much approved youug [Young].[3]

Ye brainless wits! ye baptized infidels!
Ye worse for mending! wash'd to foular stains!
The ransom was paid down, the fund of Heaven;
Heav'ns incxhaustible exhausted fund.

O why will you fatigue yourselves in the tedious round of an external form without the essence of religion, and dispise the spirit of the Lord Jesus Christ to your own eternal ruin.

Why will you reject the only thing that can sweeten your mortal days, and procure you an immortal Crown of joy and unspeakable glory? What will your labour and toil avail you, or the infinite goodness of God advantage you, if you reject and throw away the only key to all its benefits? For altho' you may think it strange, yet it is true, that when you wilfully reject, or carelesly neglect the Spirit of God and the power of the Gospel, you are crucifying Christ, murdering your own soul, increasing your chains of darkness, and cutting off every possibility of your being led to the enjoyment of that infinite ocean of goodness and love which I this day have endeavoured to unveil, or bring you to see and enjoy. O turn! turn! ye starving souls, that never have tasted of the sweets of Redeeming love, and find room in your hearts for but one drop of those rivers of pleasure!

Jesus this day proposes his leading hand, to direct your wandering minds to his courts of grace; and O ye hungry prodigals, speed your lingering return, for the Father of all mercies feels his bowels yearn over you, and is running to meet you, (k) yea and I will not tell you as many do, no I dare not, that there is no mercy with God or living bread in my Father's house for the greatest part of you; for, blessed be his name there is enough; enough, did I say? Ah! and to spare: (l) Oh! then let me take you by the hand and lead you to the full table, where you may eat, drink, and rejoice: Ah! if there is even a lame Mephibosheth, who is not only lame on both his feet, but of that rebellious house of Saul, which hath long conspired against the true heir to the Crown, he may yet come and sit and eat at the King's table, and Ziba and all his, shall be thy servants: (m) yea, and all the glorious Paradise that you lost with the first Adam shall be restored by the second, as all that pertained to Saul, was given to Mephibosheth. O be intreated to come and partake of the wonders of immortal love! for my soul feels so pregnant with an uncontainable zeal for your everlasting welfare, and your company with me to those bright mansions of my Father's bosom, that methinks I cannot be denied; for Oh! it is there, let me speak it with reverence, that I expect thro' boundless grace, when I have stood the storm of this militant state a few hours more, to share in the unspeakable privileges of the sons of God, and bear a part in

(k) Luke 15, 20. (l) Luke 15, 17. (m) 2 Sam. 9, 12, 13.

those immortal strains of praise to the glorious Emanuel; and many of this assembly I hope and expect to see among the glorious croud, who have already attained an evidence by the spirit of God sealing them to the day of redemption.[4] And Oh! methinks such of you as have been this indulged, find your hearts by this time so inflamed with love, and attracted with the glories of the approaching scene, as to constrain you to join with me and say, *O that men would praise the Lord for his goodness and his wonderful works to the Children of men!* But lest I weary the attention of those unhappy hearers, who find no sweetness in our pleasing theme, I must hasten to our fourth observation:

Which was a small discovery of the manifestations of this goodness in the preservation of this fallen family as probationers.

And here, omiting the innumerable instances of his providence to individuals, how infinite his love! how low his stoop! how hard his labour! and how unwearied his patience! in stopping the course of fallen, and nature holding the wretched family so long in such a capacity, by his incarnate spirit, as to be in a possibility of redemption! and thereby bearing the infinite weight of their contrariety, and enduring all the rage and innumerable insults of earth and hell, while at the same time he was concerting every method, and turning every stone for to reclaim them, and pouring out his favours upon them, as innumerable as the sands on the sea shore, O what love, what goodness, what wisdom, what pity, and long suffering is this! Well might the Prophet break out and say, in all their afflictions he was afflicted; and the angel of his presence saved them, in his love and his pity he redeemed them, and he bare them and he carried them all the days of old. *(n)* Ah! what sorrows, sins, pains, even in agonies of death, did this incarnate Jesus wade through! not only in the debauchery of the antedeluvian world, but even down to the day of his visible appearance! Well may God declare he was slain from the foundation of the world; *(o)* Oh! what an infinite weight must he bear, when it was by his spotless spirit that all the

(n) Isa. 63, 9. (o) Rev. 13, 8.

contrariety of the fallen system was kept from action so far as to be in a possibility of being reclaimed, when all this suppression was effected by his incarnation! And thus even the outward creature is made subject to vanity, and groans for deliverance, waiting for the redemption of the inward creature, which manifestation will bring the deliverance of the outward creature, until which the whole creation groans and travails in pain. *(p)* And thus you may see the labour, anguish, and unwearied patience of God in this preservation; and all for the good of man: Yea even what is commonly called Judgements, are wholly in love: but some of my hearers will object, How could the destruction of the Old World, Sodom and Gomorrah be in love? I answer, that neither they, nor any of the wicked are cut off, until by rejecting the offered redemption, they are gone beyond all possibility of redemption, *(q)* and therefore both in mercy to themselves and succeeding generations; for as for themselves, if you remained any longer, it would but enhance their misery; and their being cut off, sweeps away so many that are enemies to them that may be redeemed; therefore the system is divested of so much darkness and contrariety, which otherwise would have been an unspeakable obstruction to the Redeemer's kingdom.

And thus my dear hearers, you may not only understand that GOD IS LOVE, and doth all that is done upon this mortal stage in mercy, but likewise you may learn the infinite danger of remaining useless in, and an enemy to the Redeemer's kingdom.

O! awake, arise therefore ye careless and ungodly sons and daughters of Adam, ye enemies of the Lord, and stand no longer as mountains of obstruction to all that is good, no longer persist in murdering your own souls and others. O! why will you turn all the mercies of an indulgent God into chains of darkness, inflicting darts of torment and racks of despair? Or why will you persist to have your eyes evil, when his is so infinitely good? O! be entreated to think a moment on the infinite love and goodness of such a God; lay down your weapons of rebellion, confess your guilt, receive the pardon,

(p) Rom. 8, 19, 20, 21, 22. (q) Isa. 1, 5.

extoll the grace, enjoy the love, and forever adore the Name of such a GOOD GOD.

Oh! think what wisdom has been employed for you, what grace is pleading, what love is inviting, what suffering endured, what patience waiting, and what goodness surrounding you continually! Or will you still persist and despise this goodness to your own eternal ruin? will you labour to bar your hearts against the endearing charms of this melting and overflowing love?

Oh! think how much God has done, and endured for your redemption; yea and the very rocks, hills, and stones, sun, moon and stars, are all engaged for you, groaning under you, and travailing in pain for your redemption; (r) and must it all be in vain?

Must God stoop, suffer, bleed and die; grace travail, woo and plead; mercy labour, bear and forbear; wisdom propose; love court; and goodness, infinite and everlasting goodness, open the bosom of ravishing delight, and all in vain, and you at last go down into eternal ruin? Yea not only in vain, but worse, all as mountains sinking you down deeper in despair under the keen reflections, while wallowing in the bottomless gulf. Why, why O sinners, why will you abuse such love, and destroy yourselves? O! let me prevail with you to be happy, yea forever happy in this goodness, and join in one eternal thanksgiving, with songs of everlasting praise to Jehovah, for his goodness and his wonderful works to the children of men!

And now the fifth and last general observation I proceed; which was to point out some of the singular instances of the goodness of God to us in particular, but O they are so innumerable I know not where to begin!

If I speak of the gospel privileges, surely I may say that our lines are fallen in pleasant places, and we have a goodly heritage; for we came forth from the loins of our predecessors to have our trial for salvation in a day when the gospel is in its meridian brightness.

Ah! what millions have appeared for their trial in the antedeluvian darkness? millions more under but the

(r) Rom. 8, 22.

glimmering light of the Mosaic dispensations; when Oh! methinks even the poor lovers of Jesus waded in obscurity, looking through those dark types and shadows to a promised Messiah, impatiently waiting for the long expected morning, when the Messiah should visibly appear; and thousands more since he has appeared, have gone to heaven in a storm against the cruel rage of persecution, wading after their Captain in seas of their own blood; while we, with all those evidences of the truths of the gospel, are sitting under our own vine and fig-tree and none to make us afraid.

Think O my hearers, how infinitely we are indulged, invironed with the arms of omnipotence, wrapped in the mantle of love, and cultivated with the word and spirit under the balmy wing of everlasting kindness. O how largely have we been made to partake of the goodness of God, and share in the favours of his hand! and O how little returns! yea and if I come a step nearer still omiting our being excluded from heathenish darkness and from the cruelty of oppression and tyranny, how are we screened from the trials of our (once happy) Nation in the convulsions of the present day? how have we sat in peace while this inhuman war hath spread devastation thro' our Neighbouring Towns, and Colonies like a flood! not my dear hearers because of the cleaness of our hands, or past righteousness: for surely we have not only had our hands equally engaged in the sins that have incurred the lamentable disorder; but have likewise perpetrated the same crimes, and remained unfruitful and incorrigible under such distinguishing advantages.

Yea and when we have daily expected the impending cloud, and to share in the bitter cup, heaven's indulgent hand has interposed and averted the blow.

Yea, and more to be admired still we have not only been excluded from the destructive scene, but while they were involved in the dreadful calamity, we have been blest with that unparallel blessing the moving work of the Spirit of God; a work of grace, and the advancing of the Redeemer's kingdom in almost every corner of the Province; which blessed by God, (although many may and do despise it) I have been an eye witness to, and a happy partaker of; yea, and many hundreds will likewise forever adore God for the blessed Work. Neither has your little corner of the vineyard been excluded from a share in the unspeakable prize; witness some of my hearers now present who had long been involved in Egyptian darkness; has not some of your souls not only been brought out of your unhappy bondage and unspeakable danger, but likewise made to partake of God's free and boundless grace, and taste of the sweets of redeeming love? has not Jesus come into some of your families, and caused some of your souls to drink of those rivers of pleasure that makes glad the city of our God? have you not forgot your sorrows and sung for joy? O praise him then, praise him ye happy souls for his infinite goodness; or I may say in the words or our context, Let the redeemed of the Lord say say so, whom he hath redeemed from the hand of the enemy. Ye have not only been mourning in the bondage of Egypt, but have wandered in a wilderness, in a solitary way, hungry and thirsty, until Jesus appeared and led you forth by the right way to a city of habitation, where you found that rest that remains for the people of God.

O let your hearts melt with love, your souls glow with gratitude, and your minds soar away in shouts of praise of his goodness and his wonderful works to the children of men. Surely you have cause to love much, for you are blest in basket and in store, in time and eternity; for although you may be called through some trying scenes, and sometimes afflicted with losses, crosses and disappointments of this temporal world, yet it is all but to advance your spiritual welfare, and prevent greater miseries; for all things will surely terminate for your good. O you are a people highly favoured of God indeed![5] Yea, and even you that know not God, how vastly are you indulged? how innumerable are the mercies you enjoy that many cannot? Ah could I but a moment lend you an omnicient eye or discover to your view a map of the disordered world, what peals of death, what marks of misery and tokens of despair would you behold even of temporal calamities? thousands soliciting the cold hand of charity, pinched with hunger, thirst and nakedness; thousands chained to the galley, and others chain of slavery, to endure all the hardship and misery that cruelty can inflict; thousands in prisons, dungeons and places of confinement already destined to the gallows, gibbet, rack, or torture; when every pulse counts the fleeting

95

moments that crowd them with reluctance to their dreadful exit; yea, and perhaps the greatest part of those unhappy beings (too shocking for human thought) will but exchange miseries finite and tolerable, to miseries infinite and intolerable; and in a moment will find their die unalterably cast in the regions of increasing horrors and eternal despair. Good Lord, and were these once the inhabitants of the paradise of God! Ah how is the gold changed and the most fine gold become dim! *(r)* whose heart can but break and say with the Prophet, O that my head were waters and mine eyes fountains of tears, that I might weep day and night for the slain of the daughter of my people! *(s)* or how can your hearts my dear hearers but dissolve with love or break forth with thanksgiving to God for the unspeakable privileges that you are indulged with? O arise, arise and put on the Lord Jesus Christ and live to him, for he is the author and giver of all thy privileges, and is now travelling from door to door and knocking from heart to heart, for admission, and all to bring you to the fountain of all good, and the essence of unspeakable joys, yea, and he waits with unwearied patience till his head is filled with the dew and his locks with the drops of the nights. *(t)* O grant him admission, enjoy his love and live forevermore! O he calls, he calls, with arms extended to receive, you & this day (though by stammering tongue) has unvailed his goodness enough to engage your souls to love him if you would but open your hearts for the attracting view. He has not only created you in love, and came wholly in love to redeem you, but has been labouring in love for you through unspeakable miseries; and is still labouring for you, and in infinite love intreating you to partake and forever enjoy his unchangeable goodness.

And now let me in his Name reinforce the intreaties and point out your steps for to praise and adore him, and this by singularizing my hearers as in their different capacities and stations of life. And God forbid that I should point any of you to God without God; or to be christians without Christ; and therefore I am not about to lead you in a formal path of spiritless externals but an immediate application to the Lord Jesus Christ; and there to partake of that spirit and love that

(r) Lam. 4, 1. (s) Jer. 9, 1. (t) Cant. 5, 2. [Song of Solomon, 5, 2.]

will as naturally produce a christian deportment externally as fire will produce light. O therefore away to mount Calvary and drink from that bleeding love and infinite goodness which will immediately engage your souls to walk with the greatest cheerfulness in the ways of God; yea and never expect to breathe a breath to his praise or taste of his love without a saving knowledge of the Lord Jesus Christ thro' a change wrought in your soul by the spirit of God.

And if so how unfit are you to live or serve God while in the gaul of bitterness and bonds of iniquity with your souls in the darkness of your fallen state of enmity against God and all that is good.

And now let me first intreat you who are leading men of the Town[6] in Civil affairs to make it your first and chief concern to find room in your hearts for the despised Nazarene, that you who are Counsellors may be taught of God, and be as Pillars in his house, and as nursing Fathers to his people; and great, Ah? unspeakable great will be your present and everlasting reward.

Yea and great is the influence of men in your state; and as injurious as great when your ways are perverse and your examples ungodly.

Ah? what a shocking sight to see the capital men of the Earth who ought to be a Terror to evil doers, and a praise to them that do well living in sin, siting in the seats of the scornful and joining with the ungodly wallowing in vice and debauchery, & walking in luxurious paths! but god forbid that I should have any cause to suspect this to be the case with any of you present; but if it is (though I would treat you with all that respect that is due to your station and would be far from giving any wilful offence) I am under an obligation to say as Nathan to David, thou art the man; and intreat you in the Name of the Lord, and in meekness and love to return before you are landed beyond hope: for there is yet mercy at your door, and a moment more for repentance. O embrace the unspeakable privilege, and let me intreat you to adorn your station by the grace of God, and live as lights in the world, and for the Lords sake, your own souls sake, and the sake of others around you arise up and witness for God, and let all your deportment espouse the redeemers cause, and the welfare of souls.

But O! how shocking when men that should be as pillars in the house of God, and a bulwark around his fe[e]ble Lambs, are enemies to the gospel, and a wound to the hearts of his children. And Ah how shocking to see those from whose lips we might expect the dews of heaven to water and comfort the mourners in Sion, and whose Tongue should teach the songs of heaven to the rising generations, debauched with vain and obscene discourse, and belching out blasphemy? Surely says many if such men may talk and conduct so we may too. But on the other hand when they stand speak and labour for the glory of God and good of souls how would saints admire mourners rejoice and sinners Tremble!

Oh that you might be the happy instruments of such benefit to immortal souls! and great, ah unspeakably great, would be your reward; Jesus will stand by lead and support you thro' all the sorrows, labours and Trying scenes of this mortal world, give you strength equal to your day, and then receive you with a WELL DONE THOU GOOD AND FAITHFUL SERVANT ENTER THOU INTO THE JOY OF THY LORD, there to sollace in his love, Crowned with immortal glory, and forever adore him for his goodness, and his wonderful works to the children of men: but ah some of you I suppose think you would be very happy to be so blest and hope that you shall but as yet your obligations to the important affairs of your publick stations and your affinity with the carnal world, and polite age, is such, that you should greatly expose your earthly esteem and welfare for the practice or discourse much about religion. True my dear hearers you would so but let me tell you it is equally as True that unless you forsake all, you can never be his disciple, and those who are ashamed of him before men he will be ashamed of before his Father and the high angels. *(u)* therefore you may never expect to enter those bright abodes of the·everlasting day unless you are willing in this life to have your Names cast out as evil, and bear his reproach without the Camp; yea and did you see things as they really are you would account it the greatest honour that could be conferred upon you to be despised for the

(u) Mark. 8, 38.

Name of Jesus.

Ah could I a moment unvail your minds and discover to your souls one glimmering ray of the transporting beauties and resulgent glories of the Lord Jesus Christ I should have no more labour to espouse you to him, or to court you from every other love, for you would like Rebekah when courted to an unknown husband, say, I WILL GO: *(w)* Ah! you would with the greatest cheerfulness drop your earthly charms, the applause and grandeur of this vain world, and make choice of this Jesus for your present and everlasting portion, and say with the spouse, this is my beloved, and this is my friend O daughters of Jerusalem! *(x)* And then would you with gladness of heart come out and stand as a mark for the ungodly, and turn every stone, and concert every method to advance his glorious cause in the land, and to me (the few moments I am among you) would be as fellow helpers in the gospel, and with me share in the everlasting reward. O then let me again and again solicit your return from all your sinful ways and paths of vanity, and join with heart and voice to praise God for his goodness and his wonderful works to the children of men! and let the world know that you belong to Jesus. And now with God I leave you, hoping you will make the happy choice; for life and death has been set before you.

And now to every head of a family let me say, as the Lord to Zacchcus, make hast and come down for to day I must abide at thy house; *(y)* Jesus is passing by and offering to come in and make his residence with you and your families: Ah! and had you a sense of the infinite privilege of receiving the glorious visitant, you would, like the forementioned Zaccheus, come down and receive him joyfully; and say, with Joshua, as for me and my house, we will serve the Lord. *(z)* And surely my dear friends you have cause to love and adore him for his goodness to the sons of men, and to you in particular. Ah! think but a moment what miseries you have been extricated from, what dangers you have escaped, what kindnesses received, what favours enjoyed, and beyond what thousands could have expected, and beyond what thousands have enjoyed; yea if I

(w) Gen. 24, 58. (x) Cant. 5, 16. [Song of Solomon, 5, 16.] (y) Luk. 9, 5.
(z) Josph. 24, 15. (a) Lam. 3, 1. (b) Job, 16, 14.

mention no other instance but your being called away from the approaching storm that was hanging over your native land, and sheltered here from the calamities of the sweeping deluge, while many under the disolations are saying, *I am the man that have seen affliction by the rod of his wrath (a) for he breaketh in upon me with breach upon breach. (b) I am crushed as a moth, under the devastations of this inhuman war; while, saith some mourning widow in the depths of calamity, not only the partner of my life torn from my bosom, but death ravaging still, my only son, the last of all my stay, the comfort of my widowhood, is wallowing in his gore! and thus I am left nakedly exposed to all that misery and cruelty can prey, & am left to wear out the remains of a miserable life indistress of body, & anguish of soul!* And while many an aged Parent is lingering to the grave with grey hairs and sorrow, under the late news of their last son; slain in such battle, many a helpless infant is thrown an orphan into the wide world by the fatal lead destigned to the Fathers breast, while you my dear hearers (altho' you have often murmered that ever you come to those inhospitable wiles, and was ready to say with the murmering Jews *has God brought us here to slay us?* Have been hedged about with the kind providence of God, and screened from the impending storm in this peacable corner of the earth.

Yea and above all when they are thus wading thro' the terrible storm, and we have been expecting soon to share the bitter cup, we have been blest with the greatest of all blesings, cultivated with the word and spirit of divine grace, many brought to feast at the marriage supper of the Lamb, and to drink of the wells of Salvation. O the goodness, the unspeakable goodness of God to such a people, surely I may term you LITTLE GOSHEN and yet O how barren and unfruitfull are many of you still! Yea I have reason to fear that instead of prayer and praise, or your houses being as worship Temples many of you are keepers of the devils Shops, and your houses as a den of thieves, and ten hours spent in carnal mirth and sinfull pleasures to one in prayer praise or any thoughts on God and his infinite goodness; and thus your children are hurried by, and with, you the slipperly steep to eternal perdition. O the dreadfull thought! O the lamentable scene, Parents and Children all enemies to God, dispisers of Christ, murderers of souls, servants of the Devil, and bo[u]nd to the regions of eternal despair! O let me ask such Parents how can you rest? How can you linger? Or how can you be Masters of such cruelty? Or how can your hearts endure a thought of your approaching doom?

What if at your return this evening from the Sermon to your family you should find one of those children (you have led in sinfull ways) on the confines of the grave and hear them in agonies of despair saying *cursed be the womb that bear me and the paps that gave me suck and cursed be my Parents whose ungodly walk has been the means of my eternal ruin, for I am now plunging in the bottomless gulf, O that I have heard as many prayers in my Fathers family as I have Oaths but Ah I am lost my day is gone!* I say how would the shocking scene rend your despairing soul, and almost cause you to wish that you had never had a being? O then why will you any longer run the risk? Or why will thus abuse all the goodness of an indulgent God? Are you determined still to persist in your pernicious courses? And are those, all the returns that you will make for such infinite goodness endearing love and long suffering, as has this day been discovered to you?

O that I could prevail with you to return before your fatal dye is cast! Yea methinks I would creep on my knees to intreat your return if I could thereby in any degree prevail with you only to admit a serious thought and begin to bethink yourselves. O why why will you lye down in eternal sorrow? I know you will think that I Judge hard and am censorious, but if your conscience, nor the word of God, doth not condemn you neither will I; but if I have it is wholly for your own good, and God knows I speak in love with an impatient thirst for to serve you, and be a means of your everlasting happiness, that you might forever enjoy that infinite goodness, and adore God therefor.

And now to those happy Parents who under a sense of these things are returning, or have returned, and are determined by the grace of God they and their families (as far as their influence may extend) to cast themselves upon the Lord Jesus, forsake every sin, destroy every evil, and concert every meathod for the advancing the vitals of religion, and honour of God, and to exalt the Name of Jesus for his goodness and wonderfull works to the children of men; to these let me say GO ON AND THE LORD OF HOSTS WILL BE YOUR STRENGTH.

Ah it is with cheerfullness of heart I would take you by the hand and lead you on to meet and enjoy your kind Father, your helping Saviour, bleeding friend, and waiting reward. O hasten for the Lord Jehovah is inviting you with extended arms to the bosom of his everlasting love; and I know will give you strength equal to your day; and therefore altho' all earth and hell would obstruct your return yet you shall e'er long come off conquerer, yea more than conquerer thro' him that has loved you and given himself for you. O how I long to endear you to the glorious match! and methinks you will be perswaded to embrace the unspeakable prize.

Yea I am ready to say that the very thought of going hand in hand with your children to the bright abodes of everlasting day would awake in your souls an invincible resolution to arise with all your powers, fight the good fight of faith & lay hold on eternal life: say some thought full Parent some lover of Jesus can you not declare with a christian woman who (in my travails) told me that she would not care if her children were all beggars from door to door in this world if they were but walking with Christ, and she might see them at last at his right hand in glory? yea and would it not rejoice your souls to think that you should one day hear them bless God that ever they were committed to such faithfull stewards who was the means of their Salvation?

O then arise my dear Parents from your remains of sin and sloth and redouble your resolutions and prosecutions for the advancing of the redeemers kingdom in your families and let your own harmonious strains arise to Jesus for his goodness and his wonderfull works to the children of men, remembering that your unspeakable reward is present and everlasting. And now to your offspring let me say, unto you O men I call, and my voice is to the sons of men, (d) remember O remember your creator while in the bloom of life before your evil days come & the years draw nigh when you shall say ye have no pleasure in them (e) as a Servant and friend to your souls I intreat you

(d) Prov. 8, 4. (e) Revl. 13, 1.

102

while Heaven invites you, and Jesus himself is at your door knocking perswading and promising, riches and honour saith he is with me yea durable riches and righteousn[e]ss, and those that seek me early shall find me and those that find me shall find life; yea everlasting life my dear youth, with joys unspeakable and full of glory. O be intreated to leave the dangerous amusements of this vain world, turn off your eyes from beholding vanity and go in the way of understanding.

O remember what heart aching hours, scenes of sorrow miscry, and death, the bleeding Jesus had been wading thro' to save you from eternal perdition and bring you to his Fathers bosom, and can you still persist in pursuit of your Idols wallowing in your sins to the dispising of his grace, crowning him with th[or]ns, piersing his side refreshing his wounds, and plunge your own souls into eternal perdition and despair?

O be intreated to be wise in time and happy to all eternity; turn from every sin, and fly to the waiting arms of the lovely Jesus; for my part I can tell you that I was in all my earthly amusements and carnal pleasures a stranger to peace, and ignorant of a moments rest or Joy, untill I found it in this Christ that I now recommend to you; and ah I can without reluctance or shame declare myself to be one of his dispised, tho' very unworthy, followers, and recommend him to you in the presence of this auditory as a kind Master, a faithfull & loving companion, and constant helper yea altogether lovely the fairest among ten thousands, and all in all.

And by his grace I am more and more in love with him, and resolve to renew my choice of him as my only happiness and portion from this time forward and forever; yea witness God, Angels and men, witness ye Sons and Daughters of Adam present, the posts of the doors and pulpet from whence I now sound forth his Name, that by his grace assisting, I reject and abandon every lover and joy but what I may enjoy in him, and to be for him and him only, and in his Name and presence recommend to you the same choice, and declare that saints and Angels will rejoice at your return, and God himself receive you with delight. And O the unspeakable happiness you will find in him in life, and privilege in death and let me ask how would it gladen the hearts of your surviving christian Parents if they were to see you rejoicing on the confines of the grave entering the gloomy mansions of death without reluctance saying that your redeemer lived that you had known his love enjoyed his grace was now under a feeling sense of his presence, biding an everlasting adieu to all your sorrows and take your Joyfull flight to the mansion of love in your Saviours bosom?

Say some thinking Parent would you not rejoice and be ready to say that you had more Joy in the death of your child than in its birth? O be intreated then my dear young friends to bethink yourselves, fly from the Jaws of eternal perdition, and receive a crown of immortal glory, since God, angels and saints, and your own eternal welfare solicits your speedy return.

And I (of all men the most unworthy) expecting thro' boundless grace a mansion in the kingdom, long for your company to bear a part in immortal notes of praise to God for his goodness and his wonderfull works to the children of men.

And now altho' I hope each one of my hearers have been so wise as to make an application of every part of my discourse (which I thus divided to be the more striking, yet seeing a number of my fellow mortals that are in the Military establishment present I shall use the freedom to address myself to them in a few words seperately.

I am happy my dear fellow men to find those men under whose command you reside influenced to collect you to the hearing of the everlasting gospel this day, may God bless their endeavours in so doing and pour an everlasting reward into their bosom![7]

And I likewise hope your attendance is accompaniest with your own cheerfullness, and thirst for the knowledge of Christ, if so under the lest conviction of your need of the blessings of heaven O with what gladness of heart would I serve you in my Masters name, hold out to you the offers of eternal life, inviting your souls to embrace and enjoy the same; Yea altho it would not become my office to say much concerning your stations and capacity of life, yet as my fellow mortals I would as willingly serve you as my nearest and dearest friends, or the capital men of the earth; yea and as highly esteem you when your life conduct and conversation corresponds with the Gospel and principles of christianity: and would be so far from treating you with disrespect or disdain that I would at any time rejoice in that christian freedom of giving you the best advice I was capable for the good of your souls either in publick or private.

I know my dear fellow men that your souls are equally precious with my own, equally miserable by your fall, equally needy of salvation, and equally as near and dear to my blessed Master as the king, on the throne; and that you will likewise e'er long be judged by the same God, at the same impartial Bar.

O let me therefore in love to your precious and immortal souls intreat you to adhear to the offers of salvation while it is offered, embrace the Lord Jesus Christ, and live to his glory, that you may die in peace and share with the happy followers of the Lamb in the wonders of immortal Glory. You are notionally convinced that you are born to die and exposed every breath you draw to exchange worlds, and O should death overtake you unprepared you are undone to all eternity! and then what is the world and millions of worlds to you when you must lye down in the regions of eternal darkness and despair?

Yea how many have you seen (some of you) wallowing in their blood that have fell on your right hand and your left, plunged in a moment to a world of spirits (perhaps without time to ask for mercy) & doubtless many of them unprepared, and you was spared? And O did you every recollect a moment in your own breasts where you would have landed had the fatal lead have passed them and been destined to you?

Or whether you ever allow yourselves any thought of those things or not, whatever you may flatter yourselves of being saved because God is a God of Mercy, or because you expire in the cause of such and such lawful constitutions as you imagine, you let me tell you that if you die in your sins you will eternally perish in your sins; and unless you are born again, that is your hearts changed by the spirit of God you must as certainly be undone as you have a soul to save or loose. And altho I am so far from charging you with outward acts of vice and debauchery that I must acknowledge my satisfaction in scarcely hearing of a profane Oath among you as I have walked the Streets since I have been in the place, yet you are all sensible it is too commonly practised in such Corporations; yea and altho' you may any of you be guilty of that or any other vice

105

secreted from the world which may exclude you from outward disgrace or corporeal punishment, yet the crime is as heinous in the sight of that all searching eye that is about all your private paths, yea and will be not only as injurious but more so to your own souls: Because your escaping of disgrace and punishment among Men may harden you on to the commission of greater crimes to your eternal ruin: when perhaps an admonition in time might prove the means of reclaiming you and therefore my dear friends never think it any benefit to conceal your sins from men, if they are commited in the sight of God: but fly from every sin, and make it your chief concern to attain a knowledge of Christ and a life beyond the grave.

O think how shocking it is for breath that is given for repentance, and the service of God, to be spent in blasphemy, and in the service of the devil? how shocking to hear a man who is already condemned to everlasting misery, and ought to improve every breath for redemption, and to the glory of God, calling on God to damn their Bodies and souls!

O the heaven daring and soul destroying practice; God forbid that any of you should be guilty of the crime: but if there is O let me tell you in Love and pity great is their danger and e'er long unspeakable will be their misery; but if they will yet return Jesus has mercy in store for the worst of sinners; and if there if any as I hope there is among you that are seeking and enquiring after redemption, O let me take them by the hand and incourage them; Ah the Lord who has bowels of pity, and arms of love waiting to receive you will, surely give you of his holy spirit to lead you on to eternal life, if you will cast your souls on him. O fly fly my dear friends from the wrath to come and make sure an everlasting portion while there is hope. I am sensible you have never found a moment peace, rest nor sollid Joy in things of this vain world: but O in Jesus I can tell you, you will find Joys unspeakable and full of glory, O that you would be intreated to be happy for time and eternity! yea how can you refuse? I dare say if you only had the offer or any prospect of any preferment, or a commission of honour in your establishments, you would spare no pains, but break thro' every opposition, concert every method, by making all the interest that was possible to attain it. Why O why then my dear fellow men will you reject the greatest treasures and grandeur that ever was confered on any created being? Ah could you but know the rest joy and satisfaction that is to be enjoyed in Christ even while in this world you would esteem a share in his love and a humble place near his feet, far more than the crown of England! And Ah how much greater will be the joys of eternal glory where wars and runours of wars shall be no more! and O think my dear dear friends the Son of God has bled and dyed to open to your souls those bright mansions of eternal felicity, and is now yea even this day, intreating you to enter in and forever partake of the Joys of immortal light life love and Glory.

How can you forbear opening your hearts to such love and adoring him for such infinite goodness? O that I could prevail with you to carry these truths in your mind to your Barracks, and ponder them in your Sentinel hours? And I know that Jesus would be with and help you to give your hearts to him and then how happy ah unspeakably, happy would your moments glide away!

And when a few more days and nights have run their rounds, Jesus will call you from all your labours and sorrows to the joys of an eternal day, which God knows is the sincere desire of my soul, that I might see you there with all Tears wiped from your eyes, and bear a part with you, and the countless adorers in everlasting praise to God for his goodness and his wonderfull works to the children of men.

And now with a few words to the auditory I conclude.

I am happy to have an opportunity a few days my dear hearers in this part of the Vinyard to serve you, and as I speak for God with souls immortal at stake, I must without the least fear favour, or selfish ends, deliver my message, and clear my garments of the blood of souls; and altho you may many of you look on me as your enemy because I tell you the truth yet God knows it is out of love to your souls. Yea what else can you imagine would excite me to undergo the fatigues that I do both in body and mind and expose myself to all the rage of the world?

If you imagine it is for a Temporal living surely being in the prime of life I could attain what little I should need with far less Trouble; or if you imagine it is for the applause of mortals surely you may be convinced to the contrary about your own doors; for altho I have some thousands in the province that esteem me far better than I am worthy of yet you will know that I have become a song for the drunkard, & a mark for the reproaches of the ungodly world.

But O let me tell you I think both my trials and reproaches so small that the one I will hang upon my garments as ornaments to be wiped off at the glorious return of my Master, and as for the other methinks I would cheerfully undergo them again and again to see any means of bringing some of your souls to the enjoyment and everlasting, honour of the Lord Jesus Christ.

Ah I would far rather have some surviving christian passing by my tomb when I am cold in death say *here lyes the stammering tongue that taught my soul the Name of Jesus* than that they could say *here lyes the greatest earthly Monarch that ever existed.* O then let me be but a humble faithfull and successfull servant to Christ and my fellow mortals, and I have all I need; and all I desire; yea I esteem it more than millions and millions of worlds and O my dear hearers let me not be in vain to your souls but receive the message of peace the Lord hath sent by me, adore him to all eternity for his goodness to the sons of men; and I intreat you to labour with me the few moments I am in the Town for the promotion of religion, the advancing of Christs kingdom, as far as the influence of your several stations and capacities in life may extend; and may this day be not only kept as thanksgiving: but an everlasting thanksgiving kept therefore, O therefore resolve from this moment to arise from sin and sloth, and put the Lord Jesus in all your ways, love him, tell of him, walk with him, enjoy and adore him from this time forward and for ever, for his goodness and his wonderfull works to the children of men: which God of his infinite mercy grant and to his Name be the praise, AMEN.[8]

* * * * * * * * *

108

A Song of praise to a good God.
NOW let the universal throng
Unite in this eternal song
THERE IS A GOD WHOSE VAST RENOWN
DECLARES HIM GOOD WITHOUT A SOUND.

2.
Thro' all the vast immortal plains
The goodness of Jehovah reigns;
And thro' those mortal climes it rolls
From worlds to worlds, from Poles to Poles.

3.
Both Angels of exalted fame,
And abject worms declare the same,
A GOD WITHOUT BEGINING STOOD
AND EVER LIVES A GOD THAT'S GOOD.

4.
Let ev'ry insect every sand,
Rock hills and vales adore his hands!
Your being manifests a God,
And tells to man that HE IS GOOD,

5.
Ye stubborn Oaks your branches spread,
With lofty Cedars tow'ring head,
And plants and flow'rs of ev'ry hue
Proclaim A GOD OF GOODNESS too.

6.
Ye monsters of the barren wood
With your hoarse voice make known A GOD,
And troops that sail the fluid air
Join and this GOD OF LOVE declare,

7.
Ye millions of the wat'ry deep
Who spawning into being creep
Sport all your boiling mansions thro'
Proclaim a GOD ALL GOODNESS too.

8.

And rouse ye crowds of Adams race
Who share so large Jehovahs grace
While life endures or thought shall rove
Proclaim A GOD A GOD OF LOVE.

9.

Ye christian lands that own his name
The most exalted notes proclaim,
A GOD OF LOVE, INCARNATE GOD
His bleeding wounds cries out HE'S GOOD.

10.

Ye Angels blazing round the throne
(Ah ye!) where this GOOD GOD is known,
Thro' your exalted realms declare
That GOD IS GOOD, 'till we are there.

11.

When disentangled we shall land
To join with you at Christs right hand
A GOD OF LOVE shall be our theme
GOODNESS HIS NATURE LOVE HIS NAME.

12.

Long as the pow'r of thought remains
We'll praise him in exalted strains
Dive in his love but still shall own
No bounds is to his goodness known.

13.

A GOD OF LOVE! the Angels cry,
A GOD OF LOVE! the saints reply
Whoever will his love may share
GOOD GOD, and shall I not be there?

F I N I S

NOTES:

1. Simeon Perkins in his *Diary* described this sermon, preached on November 17, 1782, as "A very ingenious Discourse." Harvey and Fergusson, *Diary of Simeon Perkins 1780-1789*, p. 169.

2. This six-line poem is to be found in the New Light Letters and Songs, Acadia University Archives. It is reprinted in Rawlyk, *New Light Letters and Songs*, p. 258. In the Acadia manuscript version, the last line reads "To Reach My Jesus in the Realms above."

3. Edward Young (1683-1765) was the author of *The Complaint, or Night-Thoughts on Life, Death and Immortality* (London, 1743). It has been argued that the "vivid imagination and morbid sentimentality of Young's *Night-Thoughts*" influenced Alline's spiritual poetry. See Armstrong, *The Great Awakening*, p. 95. Alline's quotation if from Young's *The Complaint;* see his *The Works of the Rev. Dr. Edward Young* (Charlestown, 1811), Vol. II, p. 213:

   > Ye brainless wits! Ye baptiz'd infidels!
   > Ye worse for mending! wash'd to fouler stains!
   > The ransom was paid down; the fund of heav'n,
   > Heav'n's inexhaustible, exhausted fund,

   Alline did not include the last two lines on page 213:

   > And was the ransom paid? It was: And paid
   > (What can exalt the bounty more?) for *you.*

4. The "New Birth," for Alline, was the "evidence" which persuaded the believer of his or her "redemption."

5. Despite this powerful "Sense of Mission" theme in Alline's sermon Professor J.M. Bumsted has contended that "Alline did not see Nova Scotia as being particularly favoured of God, as Rawlyk and Stewart have argued." See Bumsted, *Henry Alline*, p. 106. The reader of this sermon will have to judge the merits of the two arguments.

6. It is noteworthy that Simeon Perkins, one of Liverpool's "leading men," felt that the sermon was "a very Good Discourse." Harvey and Fergusson, *Diary of Simeon Perkins, 1780-1789*, p. 169. Alline, obviously, was not preaching a revolutionary anti-elite gospel; his political and social world remained a largely deferential and conservative one.

7. The King's Orange Rangers, a small detachment of Loyalist troops, had been sent to Liverpool in 1778. They were under the command of Captain John Howard.

8. On the Acadia University Archives copy of the November 21, 1782 *Sermon* is to be found the following handwritten inscription:

> Mary Lock Dec 26 Day 1784
> Mary Lock her Book
> Given her at Liverpool
> By her friends to keep in
> her Souls friend hero
> Dead But yet Speaketh.

A
SERMON

Preached on the 19th of FEB. 1783

AT FORT-MIDWAY,

BY
HENRY ALLINE

HALIFAX. Printed by A. HENRY

Eloquent testimony to goodness of God

Classic revival Sermon

THE PREFACE[1]

SINCE the happy Moment (never to be forgotten) that Jesus deigned to Pluck me from the Jaws of Hell, and manifest his everlasting Love to my Soul by his Spirit, I have not only vowed (and still renew my Choice) to be for him only: but am (by his Grace) more and more delighted in his Truths, in Love with his Perfections, confirmed in his Gospel, and determined to walk in his Ways, and make his Name my Theme for Time and Eternity.

Let the mercenary Courters of Popularity indefatigably pursue the empty Sound of Applause, and licentious wast[e] all their Fires, and stake their whole Inheritance in a sensual Paradise; let the obscene Coquette, and self-adoring Fop, paint, powder, decorate, and (Hours at their Glass) twist, screw, turn and metamorphosis their noisious Lumps of Clay to strole about as Vassals in Quest of Eyes; let sanguine Heroes depopulate Kingdoms and wade thro' Seas of Blood to wear a Scar of Honour, and the lank-sided Miser wear out Life, starve Body, and damn Soul, to fill a Bottomless Bag: Be it my whole Portion and Labour (during my short Race cross this little World) to bear that grand Commission once given from the Throne of Heaven to Mary Magdalene (divested of seven Devils) *GO QUICKLY AND TELL THAT JESUS* (the despised *Nazarene*) *IS RISEN (a) YEA AND LIVES FOR EVER MORE!* so that it is with Delight I lend my stammering Tongue, and unpolished Pen, at every Opportunity to labour in, and exhibit the glorious Theme.

And therefore when requested by my Friends who were present (almost every Person in the Place) when this Sermon was delivered, I hand it to the press (with some small, but usefull Alterations)[2] for their further Benefit, and the good of Others; and may God bless the glorious Truths, hand them O Jesus by thy Spirit to the Heart of Thousands, to their Joy and thine eternal Praise, AMEN.

(a) Matt. 23, 7.

SERMON
From Gen. 37, 16. *I seek my Brethren*

O what Stones have been turned! What Mountains moved what Methods concerted! What Labour and Miseries endured by Jehovah himself to seek and save a lost World! How doth he Travail, call, knock, wait, woo, and beseech, with unwearied Patience, to save Mankind from Misery and Despair, and bring them to Joy and unspeakable Glory! O, the infinite Love of that despised Jesus, which you have heard me so often since I have been with you, (and will again) recommend to you my poor, guilty, starving, perishing and undone fellow Mortals!

How hath he stooped from his Realms of immortal Glory, waded thro' the Disorders of your miserable World in the Agonies of Death and Miseries of Hell, with his Vesture dipped in Blood, travelling from Kingdom to Kingdom, from Town to Town, from Village to Village, for to seek his Brethren; knocking from Heart to Heart with bleeding Hands, and an aking Heart, till his Head is filled with the Dew, and his Locks with the Drops of the Night! yea, and this Night (tho' by a stammering Tougue) is come to your Doors calling on Sinners, and saying in the Words of our text, *I SEEK MY BRETHREN*, which by his Assistance is to be my subject and employ in his Name this evening by endeavouring to exhibit a glorious, clear and effecting Type of Christ, and shall much insist on Christs seeking his Brethren: But before I proceed to follow the Chain of Typical Histories, I would first speak a few Words to guard the Minds of Sinners from any Injury from my useing with them the Word Brethren, a Term which I shall often make use of, being the Language of our Text; for altho' Christ declares his Disciples not to be Servants, but Brethren, which may likewise be applied to the unregenerate: But not in that Sense as to his Children; Sinners or the unregenerate Part of the World are so far related to Christ as to be held up by him in Flesh and Blood by his becoming Flesh, and thereby likewise they stand in a Possibility of becoming his inseparable Brethren, which he is labouring for: Yet while in an unregenerate State they are not his Brethren as his children are; yea are so far from it that altho' he calls them Branches, yet

115

they are exposed every moment to be cut off and cast into the Fire; *(b)* their standing thus in Flesh and Blood are so near related to Christ, that by his incarnate Spirit they are restrained from that immediate Destruction which they would plunge themselves in, if left to act themselves: But they can never bring forth any Fruit unto God untill they have given up the Heart, for the will to act with Christ; and therefore you that are strangers to Conversion may be so far from flattering yourselves with the Name of Christians or Christ's Brethren, that you have cause to tremble at the Thoughts of remaining so long at emnity against him, and the infinite Danger of your being cut off in a Moment from all Relation to him, or Benefit by him, and be consigned over to the miserable State of his most inveterate Foes. O, therefore, let me intreat you, as you love your own souls, if Christ (as he realy is) is now seeking after you to adhear to his Calls, be found of him, and forever enjoy him; and be his Brethren and Companions to all Eternity.

And now to convince you of his Willingness to save you I shall endeavour to discover his Love, Goodness, free Grace, Labour, and Longsuffering, and Willingness to save you, in the Life and Conduct of Joseph, who in my Opinion is the most clear, glorious and effecting Type of Christ, that all divine Revelation affords us. First, he was his Father's beloved Son, the darling of his Bosom: and nothing less, O my hearers, than God's only begotten Son, the darling of his Bosom, and beloved of all Heaven, was the Seeker and Saviour of a lost World; nor could all the Armies of Heaven, if engaged on the important Errand have got one Soul home to immortal Glory: Because nothing could effect the Work, but that wrought in them, which none, but God would possibly effect.

Think, O! Ye Sons and Daughters of Adam, what a Stoop of Jehovah for you and me! and was it for us? and are you the People that he came to seek! Yet, saith our Text, and the whole Gospel, to every soul present, this evening *I SEEK MY BRETHREN!* O let him not seek in Vain. Again Joseph has hated of his Brethren, and set as a mark for all their Rage,

(b) John, 15, 2.

116

Malice and Cruelty: And, O! by woeful Experience, I know that the carnal Mind is at Enmity against the Lord Jesus Christ, not subject to his Laws, neither indeed can be. Ah! and by woefull Experience he knew what it was to stand as a mark for all the Malice of Earth and Hell! and when he came to his own, his own received him not. Neither imagine my Dear Hearers, that those ungodly Men only, who had their Hands engaged in his corporeal Punishment and temporal Death, were the only hands in his Misery, or men enraged against him: for your Sins not only pierced his Soul then, but likewise are still at Enmity against him now; and while you do not find Room for him in your Heart, and yeild your whole Soul into his Hand, you are among his Enemies, and are declaring, that you will not have this Man, to reign over you. O Sinners awake, and for your soul sake, look about you before your loss is irreparable! Again, Joseph incured the Malice and Displeasure of his brethren in a greater degree, because he foretold them what would come to pass: So the Jews and all the wicked are the more enraged against Christ, because he foretells them; what will come to pass: for he came to bear Witness to the Truth, which he maintained in the very Agonies of Death; throw down, O! Sinners your weapons of Rebellion, and love him, for *he is the Way, the Truth and the Life.* And when Joseph's brethren were keeping their Flocks in the Field his Father called upon him to go and look after them; *go, saith Jacob, and see what is become of thy Brethren,* if it be well with them, so when we were *wallowing in our Blood, cast out in the open Field to the loathing of our Persons,* or as the Man fallen amongst thieves, *striped, wounded, and left half dead* without any help from the Law or its Executors, the Father of all Mercies calls upon his only Son to look after us; go, saith God, my Son, my only Son, my Delight, my Joy, my Life, my all, and seek thy Brethren; look after thy Creatures, the wreched miserable and lost Family of Adam. And O! Shall I tell you my Hearers, he cheerfully obeys! Ah! it *was a Time of Love* indeed! Hark! and you will hear him say, *LO, I COME IN THE VOLUME OF THY BOOK OF LIFE TO DO THY WILL O GOD: (c) I WILL CAST MY SKIRT OVER THEM AND SAY UNTO THEM, LIVE.(d)* And this Night, O

(c) Heb. 10, [7]. (d) Eze. 16, 6.   117

Sinners, he is come to seek you and wraps you in the Mantle of his free Grace: O believe and live for ever; for Jesus is come to enquire after you, or will you like Joseph's Brethren, say, *here comes that filthy Dreamer!* Will you reject his Calls, despise his Offer, abuse his Love, and destroy yourselves to all Eternity? I imagine you will blame Joseph's Brethren, and think they were divested of all the Movings of Conscience, and abandoned to all the Dictates of Humanity, for to conspire against him, when they saw him coming; and yet you will be guilty of conspiring against the innocent Lamb of God, thy Soul's best Friend and only Helper, when coming for your Good: Joseph perhaps was likewise loaded with some Refreshment or Temporal good Things to nourish them from his Father, which he gladly carried to support and comfort his Brethren, yet they could say, *here comes that filthy Dreamer; let us now lay Hands on him and destroy him, and see what will become of his dreams:* and so when the Sinners friend was come, and (if I may say in our common Language) with his Arms full of Bread, and loaded with good cheer for his starving, miserable, and perishing Brethren, the Jews and all the Ungodly can cry out *this is the Heir, let us fall on him and kill him; this is he that hath pretended to be King, we'll destroy him, and see what will become of his Kingdom; this is he who saith he can build the temple in three Days, and that he is the Son of God; if he is, let him come down now from the cross; if Elias be his friend let us see if Elias will come and help him.*

And will you, O! my Hearers, persist in such Cruelty, and perpetrate the horrid Murder? O! be wise, be wise, have mercy upon yourselves, embrace the despised Nazarene, escape eternal Perdition, and be everlastingly happy; for *Jesus* is come, knocks at your Door, and cries with a loud voice, *I SEEK MY BRETHREN,* and take heed to yourselves my Dear Hearers, that you do not hug Unbelief, that Murderer, and reject him while I am speaking, But to return to our Type of the Messiah, they cast him into a Pit untill they saw a Company of Ishmaelites travelling from Mount Gilead, and then they took him out and sold him for Twenty Pieces of Silver; And O! must it be told, that the eternal Jehovah was Sold for but Ten more! O! Tremble ye Judas like Lovers-of-money! And bethink yourselves of your Danger, lest you sell

118

your souls and an interest in the eternal kingdom of Grace and Glory for a few Ounces of Dust.

O Leave, leave your bewitching God's before they have bewildered your poor deluded Souls to the howling Mansions of Blackness and Despair. Why will you run the Risk of loosing a Soul immortal for that which can neither abide with you, nor make you happy while you possess it? You may think perhaps you are not guilty of that Lust for Gold as to sell Christ and loose your Soul for it: But let not the Devil deceive you my dear Hearers; for if the most simple Pleasures, inoffensive Enjoyments, or lawfull Concerns (as you call them) of this Life, engages your Attention, and amuses your Mind so as to keep you from giving up your whole Soul to God and making the Lord Jesus Christ your chief Good, you are as guilty of Idolatry as Micah, as guilty of selling Christ, as Judas, and therefore without Repentance will soon be as miserable; for the soul-rending Moment approaches when all these your Amusements will be eternaly swept away, and consequently you must immediately be in keen Despair; for like Micah you will say, ye have taken away my God's, and what have I more? O! Be intreated to open your doors this night for the waiting Jesus, and you will have God that will live and stand by you forever.

But again, to return, *Joseph* was soon for his Purity and Chastity (for I must omit many passages of his life) a Prisoner between the Butler and Baker: so was the Spotless Son of God for his holiness, purity and Truth, a prisoner between two Theives, who were justly condemned, but he unjustly, and as one of *Joseph's* fellow Prisoners suffered death, so one of the Thieves blasphemed the God that made him and sunk in eternal Death; while as Joseph told the Butler he should be brought to the King's Table to serve with the Cup of Wine, the other Thief cries, *Lord remember me when thou comest into they kingdom,* and Jesus told him that he should that same Day be with him in Paradise; *(e)* Ah, where he rejoices at the King's Table, and drinks of living Wine forever! O! be incouraged then ye condemned Souls, who like the expiring

(e) Luke 23, 43.

Thief are just bidding this mortal World an everlasting Adieu, there is yet hope; Jesus is yet alive; Ah, and as near you as he was to the dying Criminal, and as boundless in his Mercy: But, O, Remember the other Theif went to Hell with a Christ as nigh. O! What a dreadful thought to go down to everlasting Perdition so nigh the gates of Heaven, and sink to Hell with Salvation at the Door! But I must return, and likewise entreat your most engaged Attention with me to the Type reflecting therefrom to the Glorious Anti-Type. Joseph is soon exalted to the second person in the Kingdom, and in a Time of Famine has the care and command of all the gran [grain] in Egypt, so that if any came for Bread, Pharaoh told them to *go to Joseph:* And O! I can tell you, you that find like the prodigal Son a Famine in the Land, and begin to be in want, that Jesus, my blessed Master, whom you have sold to the Ishmaelites, is become, yea, and always was God over all blessed for ever more, and turns (if I may use such Language) the Key of all the Heavenly Granary; let me therefore say to you as the Patriarch to his starving Sons, *why sit ye here looking sad one upon the other? behold I hear there is corn in Egypt, get ye down and buy for us, that we may live and not die. (f)*

Why sit ye here, O ye starving Sons and Daughters of Adam, perishing for lack of bread, when Jesus is yet alive and in your Brothers house, there is bread enough and to spare?

O Arise! Arise, and go down to Egypt, and buy without Money and without Price! *but why,* saith one, *or how in Egypt, when I thought that Egypt, in a spiritual Sense, signified a State of Death, Darkness and Bondage? Or the unconverted State?* True, my dear Hearers it does, and yet ye must go down to Egypt nevertheless for to get bread for your starving Souls; that is, see yourselves thus in Egypt; and not only so, but the corn is realy in Egypt, as soon is ever the Sinner finds himself there; and therefore ye need not say, who shall ascend up to Heaven to bring you down the bread of Life, nor into the Deep, for the Bread of Life is nigh you, even in your hearts, so that if you will but believe ye shall eat and live, yea and rejoice for evermore. *(g)*

(f) Gen. 42, 2. (g) Matt. 15, 20.

And now to a further review of our typical Subject, we find the Sons of Jacob going down with their Money to Egypt for to get Corn; and let it never be forgotten, my Hearers, that not one farthing of their Money was taken: but all returned; each one with his loaded Sack and his Money in the Sack's Mouth.

Ah! a glorious truth for the Poor! Learn hence, that altho' Pharisee like, we may labour hard to wash our Hands before we eat, and thereby carry our imagined Cleaness, good Duties, and strict Performances to recommend ourselves to God; or speaking vulgarly to buy Bread, Yet after all we have done, whoever attains one Crum of the Bread of Life will receive it as a Gift with their Money all returned. And blessed be God he has told us it will not defile a Man to come to the Gospel Feast and eat with unwashen hands! *(g)* O! Come then ye starving (or rather proud) Sinners, just as you are, and cease from that Custom, which was among the Pharisees, and is still; yea, spread over almost all Christendom, and practiced in the Heart of almost all professors, to wash before they eat, or prepare themselves to come to Christ; cease, I say, from the God-dishonouring and Soul-destroying Practice, and come to Jesus as you are; with all your Sins, and in all your Vileness; Ah! without Money and without Price; for Jesus, who cannot be benefited by any of your Mercenary Services, invites you to a full Table. Hark, hear the glad news! *GO YE AND LEARN*, saith he, *WHAT THAT MEANETH, I WILL HAVE MERCY AND NOT SACRIFICE;* and therefore *EAT O FRIENDS, DRINK, YEA DRINK ABUNDANTLY, O BELOVED, FOR THE SON OF MAN CAME NOT TO BE MINISTERED UNTO, BUT TO MINISTER, AND TO GIVE HIS LIFE A RANSOM FOR SINNERS, AND WHEN WE WERE WITHOUT STRENGTH, IN DUE TIME CHRIST DIED FOR THE UNGODLY;* observe the Words, my dear Hearers, not for the Godly, but *FOR THE UNGODLY:* And therefore, for your Soul sake, do not bar yourselves out of Heaven with your faithless Prayers, Spiritless Duties, and Christless Christianity: But go, like Mephibosheth, lame in both feet to the King's Table.

But, saith one, would you not have us pray before we come to Christ? yes, my dear Hearer, if there is any Danger of getting to Christ too soon. But saith one again, must we not pray to get to Christ? I answer yes, if you can pray without Christ, or get to heaven without Christ, or by your prayers recommend yourself to Christ.

But let me tell you, that, think what you will of your prayers, if ever you come to Christ, they will be all taken away, and you will come to him without one Prayer, form or Duty, to recommend you; yea, if you have already prayed seven Years, and should live to add seven Years more of such Prayers, you may never expect to receive Christ untill you have left them all, and come to Christ without one of them. And now what think you my dear hearers of making a Ladder of your Prayers, or of staying away from Christ until you have prayed more? Christ must be a whole Saviour at last if ever you receive him, and therefore why not receive him as a whole Saviour now? you may think perhaps that I am overseting all Religion by speaking so much against your Prayers: but let me tell you, that you will never know or enjoy one Spark of True Religion, untill all those recommending prayers are overset. For altho' you may excuse yourself that you do not depend on your Prayers, nor in the least degree expect to recommend yourself to God by all your Duties, or all that ever you can do; yet you are so far deceived that I can prove you are so far depending on them (I mean you that are awakened and seem to be seeking after Salvation) as to keep yourselves from Christ thereby; yea, and it is the bar that keeps you this moment from casting yourselves on him; for was you strip[p]ed of those false Supporters, you would immediately cast yourselves wholly on the Mercy of God, and would soon be rejoicing in Jesus Christ, the God of your Salvation; which to convince you of, let me only ask you a few Questions.

Some of you I am sensible by the private Discourse I have had with you, begin to be convinced of your lost and undone Condition, and have been forsaking your Sins, evil practices, and carnal Amusements, and are daily, yea, some hourly, seeking after Christ by your Prayers, and labouring to have your Souls converted; well, and let me ask you further, have you not been determining of late to be more engaged and faithful in the Means of Grace, or in pursuit of Conversion, than ever you have been? Yea, are you not this very Moment,

122

while I am speaking, concluding and resolving in your Minds, that you intend to begin your lives Anew, and if you live ever to get home, or till the ensuing Day, or Week, you will be more engaged than ever you have been, and pray more, and pray oftener than you have done? And pray, what is all that determination of Amendment of Life, new Resolutions, engagedness of Seeking, more Earnestness of Prayer, and more repeated cries for? Is it not all to attain Conversion with, and thus to recommend you to Christ? for if you did not think you would get nigher to him, and more prepared for his Grace, or more likely to attain Conversion thereby, you would not do it. And thus, I dare say, you have some of you got a Week's Work to compleat in your Mind to bring you to Christ, or to do before you expect to find him, yea and some of you a Month's or a Year's Work, that you intend to do before you expect to find him. And now, my dear Hearers, if this be the truth of the Case with any of you, which I dare say, it is, how can you say, you have got no Selfrighteousness, or any Thing that you depend on, or expect to recommend you to God, when you have not only got what you have done, laid up in your Mind, but intend to get much more before you are converted, or before you will come to Christ? do you expect that God will be more mercifull some Weeks or Months hence, than he is now? Or do you expect, that by doing all that you have designed, you will prevail with him to give consent, that you should be saved? or (as I would put the most favourable Constructions that I can on your Designs) finding a hard Heart and stubborn will, do you expect thereby to soften the Heart, and bow the Will? if not, if none of these are your Designs and expectations, then, why would you persue such steps, or why are you not willing to receive the Mercy of God now? if you must as last come to Christ with a hard Heart, and all your Sins why are you not willing to cast yourselves on him now? And why are you not convinced now my Dear reader,[3] by these arguments, that you are endeavouring to buy Salvation, and that you are not willing to receive Christ on his own Terms, or his Grace as a free gift; altho' he is now come to seek you. But saith one again, what would the man have us do? Would he have us neglect Praying, and all our duties? I answer, my dear Hearers, if you have accepted of Christ, you have neither prayed nor

123

discharged one Duty, either to the Glory of God, or the Good of your own Souls; and therefore, I am so far from advising you to cease from Duties and Prayers, that I intreat you to perform them immediately, and that by taking Christ with you; for without him I have proved, that you never have, nor ever can, either pray or perform the least Duty acceptable to God, or to the Good of your own Souls, and therefore if your Days should be lengthened out to the Age of Methuselah and all wore out in performing those Duties and prayers, which you have prescribed, or resolved upon in your own Mind, you would not be one step nearer to Christ, or any more prepared for Conversion, than you are now; and therefore what think you now of staying away from Christ any longer to be prepared to come or of praying and performing duties with Christ? but saith one, what would the Man have us do, we cannot convert ourselves, nor think that God will convert us now, or bring us to rejoice in Christ this Evening? to which I reply, you may convert yourelves (if I may use such language) as well now as the next Year, or Ten Years hence; and if you cannot convert yourselves neither now nor then, but God must do it for you; is not God as able and willing to do it now, as he will be To-morrow, next Year, or the Year after, or any Time to come? yea, and let me tell you, that, altho' you have often been taught, and often said, you would and must wait God's time (which is the very language of the Devil) and so put it off for some future Period! Yet God declares, that his Time is now; *now is the acceptable Time and to Day is the Day of Salvation;* yea, let me tell such People, that God has been long waiting your Time, and waited in Vain, and if you should putt him off so a few Days more, your Day will be over, your Time at a Period, your Soul gone, and your Loss irrecoverable; and then it may be said by God, *I called and ye refused, I stretched out my Arm and ye regarded not, I therefore will laugh at your Calamities, and mock when your Fear cometh.*

O! therefore, as you love your own Souls, put off a waiting Saviour no longer, lest you loose your Soul to all Eternity. You say you cannot think that God will convert, or bring your soul into Liberty this evening, and yet, I dare say you expect he will some other Time, and this is the very thing still that keeps you from him: For he never can, nor never will be your Saviour until you, not only believe he is able and willing, but so far believe it the present moment, that you will cast yourself on him without any expectation of a future opportunity; yea, you must and will be reduced to such Extremity, that you can no longer be put off, or any way pacified with or resting upon, what may, or will be done at some other time, or hereafter, but will in immediate extremity, cry like sinking *Peter* for help now, *Lord I cannot live any longer without thee, save me, yea save me immediately, or I sink forever.* And then, my dear Hearers, and never till then, will you receive the waiting Saviour; so that by this Time, methinks you must be convinced, that you have been (under a pretended Reverence and Humility) puting off the Lord, like Felix, for a more convenient Season, and thereby baring yourself from Salvation, and thus saying, that you cannot come yet, and cannot believe yet: but you hope you shall by and by, or some other Time; which is the strongest Terms saying, that you will not believe yet, nor you will not come yet, but by and by, or some other time when you have got some better Frame, you will come: but let me tell you my dear Hearers, wait and try what you will, and as long as you will for a better heart, a softer heart, a loving heart, a humble heart, or a broken heart, and a better Frame, you will be after all, but like the Woman who was Twelve Years trying many Physicians for a Cure till she spent all her living, and instead of growing better grew worse, and was obliged at last to press thro' the Crowd with all her Disorders, and touch the hem of Christ's Garment, or never be made whole, yea, and if ever you are healed, you must like her not only despair of all other Helps and Physicians: but be reduced that to perishing Extremity, that you will press thro' the Crowd of every Temptation and disagreeable F[r]ame to Jesus the last Resource, and complete Saviour.

     O believe that you are as fit, and as worthy to come to Christ now as you will be if you Labour and mourn and pray all your Days, and that the Lord Jesus Christ is now waiting to receive you! O believe that the great Jehovah offers you Salvation this moment as a free Gift. *But saith one again, must I come to him just as I am now with a hard Heart, dark Mind, and polluted Soul?* I answer yes. Nor will it ever be any better untill you do. You may court the Terrors of the law, and the awful Apprehensions of Death and the Grave, together with a dismal Discovery of the Pains of Hell, and the dispairing Horrors of the damned, which indeed may alarm some careless Sinner that has never been roused scarcely to a Thought of his miserable Condition before: But those who have been long awakened by the Spirit of God, and under a sense of their Danger, there is nothing will effect them, but to cast themselves on God, and feel His love and Goodness. And therefore instead of your going to Mount Sinai to soften the Heart after you have seen your lost undone Condition, I would point you to that infinite Love, and Goodness that so freely bled beneath your Sins, and threw open the Gates of eternal Glory for the vilest of the Vile; and therefore ye need not go any longer *to the Mount which burneth with Blackness and Darkness and Tempest, and to such Thunderings and Lightnings that made even Moses and all the Hebrew Camp to Tremble; which Mount, if so much as a beast touch was thrust thro' with a Dart:* but ye may and ought to *come to Mount Sion, the City of the living God, the heavenly Jerusalem, and to an innumerable Company of Angels, to the general Assembly and Church of the First Born which are written in Heaven, and to God the Judge of all, and to the Spirits of just Men made perfect;* And O shall I tell you! *to Jesus the Mediator of the new Covenant.* Ah, *and to the Blood of sprinkling,* my dear hearers, *that Speaks better Things,* yea, far better, *Than the Blood of Abel;* and all this a free Gift, to whoever will, may enter and enjoy the glorious privileges forever: but these blessings you can never attain, but by ventureing on Christ. And now think a Moment (ye that mourn a hard Heart) that all this was the Price of Blood for you, Ah! for you in particular; yea, and the same Friend that has done all this, will do and grant all that you need; yea, so willing to make you everlastingly happy, that he not only offers it to you, but his heaviest Complaint and greatest grief is, that even after all he has done for you, ye will not believe him, nor enjoy it; and he mourns because of your Danger still, or mourns shall I say, because his Labour is all to you like to be lost, and you, after all the pains he has endured forever abandoned to all that is good, banished from his presence, and lay down, in the Regions of

126

eternal Darkness and Despair: but if you cannot believe this step with me a Moment to the Gates of that bloody City where you will see him weeping over a People, that by rejecting his Grace have chained themselves to irrecoverable ruin and Despair, even when thus gone, and that against all that he had done, or could do, yet he feels their Misery, and condoles their State with a bleeding Heart, in Words that might cause any Hardness, but that of Sin or final Impenitence to melt; *he beheld* saith God, *the City and Wept over it*, Ah, wept over it indeed! *saying, if thou hadst*, or, O that thou hadst! *Known at least in this thy Day the Things that belonged to thy Peace, but,* Ah, by rejecting now, *they are* to my almost insupportable Grief, *hid*, for ever hid *from thine Eyes!*

Yea, so great was his Pity, that, if it had been possible, he would yet have brought them to Repentance, if his labouring Years longer would have done it: laboured Years longer, did I say? Ah, I am so far from charging God, as many do with designing the Misery of them that are lost, or consenting to their Ruin, that is permit them to be ruined when he could have prevented it, neglecting to save them when he could, I say instead of believing so, I as firmly believe, as I believe there is a God, that his Love is so great, his Goodness so uncontainable, that if any more of the fallen Race, could be redeemed by his suffering more for them, he would with as much Freedom as he once gave his life, when no man took it away, *(h)* enter again in the Flesh, and undergo all the unspeakable Miseries again, even to Death, for such is the nature of the Divine Being, as can never be roiled, incensed, or stirred up to thirst for Revenge tho' a Truth, which I have been condemned for declaring: yet a Truth that I am more and more willing to vindicate by the infallible Word; Yea, and a Truth that I trust, I shall believe and rejoice to all Eternity. but saith one of my Hearers, *I thought God was nothing else but Vengeance against the Ungodly, and angry with the Wicked every Day.* True, my dear Friends, he is as Vengeance to the finally Impenitent, because of sin: But you must not imagine this Vengeance or Anger, so called to be any Thing that is so in

(h) John 10, 18.

God, or awoke in God since the Sin was committed, or any Thing that is Wrath or Vengeance in itself; but so to the wicked by Reason of the infinite Contrariety of their Guilt and Sin; and thus it is, that he is angry with Sin from the Consequence of his Nature, that is, and forever was so opposite to Sin, that they can no more abide together than Light and Darkness, Heat and Cold; but when Light scatters Darkness, would you imagine therefrom, that the Light was possessed of Malice, Spite or Revenge against the Darkness? or when fire dissolves the Ice will you say, that the Fire was incensed by the Ice? or mad with the Ice? Why then will you imagine, that God is roiled, incensed, or got a Wrath and Spirit of Revenge stirred up in himself against Sin, because he hates and abhors Sin? Or why would you say, that he was possessed of Wrath, and Vengeance against the Sinner, because his nature is so to them, while in their Sins when at the same Time his Nature in itself is all Love and Goodness? but some may say again, if God is never roiled nor incensed, why does he cast the Sinners to Hell at all? I answer, my dear Hearers, he never does: for they by Sin make their own Hell and go to their own Place.

But perhaps you will say again, I know they so far make and go to their own Hell that they justly deserve it, and therefore God's Throne is clear of their Blood: but yet I think he could still save them if he would: but as they have so often and willfully rejected, he swears they *shall not enter into his Rest.* And now, as that is the Conception of many, who are called Christians, I shall speak a few words more in answer whereby I shall discover the horrible Consequences of that Principle, first if that was the Truth, then God is changeable, for when he first calls the Sinner, he is not got that Wrath and Vengeance against him: but by the Sinners rejecting the Calls, he stirs up a Wrath and incenses a Justice, which never can be appeased or satisfied. Secondly, he is not only less mercifull now, then he was before the Sinner rejected his Mercy: but likewise possessed of something incensed, or some Wrath and Anger, as long as the Sinner lyes in Hell, which God never would have felt or been possessed of, if the Creature had not sinned; so that consequently not only the Creature, but God too is injured by Sin to all Eternity; which you see must be the case (let people twist and turn as much as they will to cover

128

their Dark and unscriptural Sentiments.) And now what think you my dear Hearers of such blasphemous Conceptions of the Deity as many have and hold forth as the truths of the everlasting Gospel? Yea, and will level all their Artillery against any one who presumes to believe in any better God, or who discovers the nature of their Principles: But, blessed be God, I feel more and more delighted with, confirmed in, and impatient to proclaim that glorious truth with the beloved Disciple, *God is love*, yea, *he is light*, saith the same John, *and in him is no darkness at all.* O my hearers, fall in love with such a God! a God whose Nature is so good as to exclude him from any possibility of feeling or doing any thing but good; Yea a God, that will labour to do good as long as the Creature is in a Capacity of receiving; nor will ever give the Creature up to misery, untill he is gone beyond Recovery; stepping in himself, and saying *what could have been done more, that I have not done?*

But saith one, doth not this Doctrine of God being all Love and Goodness open a Door to licentiousness, and tend to harden Men to go in Sin, and put off their Repentance? I answer, it is so far from having that Tendency, that it is the most invincible Bulwark against it; as I will convince you in a few Words. For if the Creature's Salvation could be effected by an arbitrary Act of God at any Time and their Damnation turned upon his being awoke to Anger and Resentment and Revenge; then God can and may send them to hell whenever he please if they labour ever so much to attain his Favour, and on the other Hand, he may save them whenever he please if they live in Sin ever so long, yea may force them into Heaven, even if they live and die in their Sins and Rebellion, and therefore, if the Salvation and Damnation of the Creatures turn thus, what need have they to put their Hearts to the Work, or trouble their Minds about Salvation at all? but when you declare to them (as the Truth realy is) that altho' God is nothing but Love and Goodness, yet if they do not improve their Day of Probation immediately, they may the next moment (and certainly will soon) be so sealed up in final Impenitence within themselves as to be beyond the reach of an Omnipotent Arm; and then that love and goodness will be so far from doing them any good, that it will be their greatest Torment; for the Love, Goodness and purity of God will be to their hellish Nature, as Oyl to the Fire, increasing the Flame Yea and when thus gone, are not gone, because God was Angry, and rose up against them in Revenge, but are become in themselves such as God cannot help no more than he can change; yea and have become such as the nature of God was forever opposite to, and forever will be, and therefore as his Nature will forever augment their misery they must forever endure unspeakable Torments thereby; for he can neither change nor cease; and as long as he exists his Presence and Nature will be to them an unspeakable Addition to Torment and Misery. And thus my dear Hearers, I have discovered to you the Reason why Sinners may be eternally lost and miserable, altho' God is (without change) all Love and Goodness; a God of Love and goodness indeed. Ah, and so far from being stired up to seek Revenge, that, altho' like Joseph's Brethren, ye have been guilty of murdering your innocent and best Friend, yet his bleeding Heart is open still to receive you. Ah, see him thro' all the Agonies of a miserable Life, labouring for the good of his inveterate Enemies! yea, and in the last Agonies of Life, while so crushed with the infinite Weight of their Rebellion, that his Soul was racked with the accute Tortures, and groaning under the insupportable Burden, he was so far from being roiled, incensed, or stired up to Resentment, or Revenge, by all their Insults and Cruelty, that his last Groans was *Father forgive them:* but O! What was that he said? Think, O my soul! and let me repeat the Words, *Father forgive them*, he says: Hear, O Sinners, and feel, the affecting prayer; the last groans of thy best Friend, and O he dies! Ah he dies! and for whom? Why for you and me. Dies, did I say? Yes, he dies: yet he lives, and lives forevermore; *and where's a God so good?* this night, O sinners under our roof, and near thy Heart; yea, blessed be his Name, methink's, I have some feeling Sense, I will not say as is commonly said, his awfull Presence, no: but his allglorious sweet and soulravishing Presence: but so rapid has the divine Truths flowed into my Soul, that perhaps I am tedious, I therefore return, and come now to the most effecting Passage of our Typical Scene. Joseph's Brethren being found with the King's Cup! and brought back therefor as Thieves Traitors, refreshes in their memory the horrid crime once committed against their inocent Brother, which now stares them in the face and causes every Groan and Feature to betray the Horrors of a guilty Conscience, and the Anguish of an almost despairing Soul.

O! say then, one to the other, *all this has befallen us on Account of our Cruelty to our Brother; and Vengeance hath thus pursued and overtaken us, because that we thus slew him, and refused to Pity.*

Ah! now we remember the Anguish of his Soul, the Beating of his bleeding Heart, and the Groans of his distressed Breast when our Hands were abandoned to all the Dictates of Humanity, our Souls divested of Compassion, and our Hearts abdurate against the melting Intreaties of his wounded Soul! and what now shall we do? For our Iniquities have overtaken us, and by the Cruelty of our Hands we are hedged upon every Side! O! wretched Men that we are! For the Day of our Calamity is come! And we are excluded from every Helper, and cut off from every Prospect of Hope! We are destined to Misery by every aggravating Circumstance, for every thing conspires our ruin, augments our Miseries! We have not only left our aged Parents under the Distresses of a cruel Famine, but to lash on their speedy declines of Life, and crush their exhausted Frames with the Agonies of all that loss can prey.

"Ah! well may they say, when they hear of our hard fate, Joseph is dead! Benjamin is not! and the rest where are they? And thus in the Bitterness of Soul and anguish of Heart, we shall indeed ring their gray Hairs with Sorrow to the Grave!

But Joseph, who understands their Language, without an Interpreter, can forbear no longer, O! saith he within himself, *how can I endure any longer to hear the Groans of their sinking Spirits, or stand against the humble Acknowledgments of their Cruelty to me! O! I feel the Sighs and Groans, of their bleeding Hearts, and almost despairing Souls, my Breast throbs, my Bosom burns, my Heart akes, and my whole Soul is dissolved with melting love, and uncontainable Compassion for my poor distressed and brokenhearted Brethren! and so pregnant is my Bowels with Compassion that my labouring Soul wants vent for the Sympathy I feel O! Hand me to my bedchamber, that I may give vent to the Convulsions of my sympathizing Bosom!*

131

Alone he weeps; and Ah, did his Brethren know how would it mitigate their Sorrows, expell their Fears, and ease their desponding Souls of their almost insupportable Burdens! Well, soon they'll know: — but let me leave them a moment and view the trembling Sinner, when apprehended if I may so say? And found with the King's Cup, how do they shrink when under the Thunders of Mount Sinai! they begin to discover the Folly, the Rebellion, the Cruelty, Theft and Murder, that they have been guilty of. Ah! says the convicted soul, with a trembling Conscience, *I have rebelled against Heaven, I have deserted from God, stole, carried away and converted like Belshazzer, the Vessels of the House of the Lord to an evil Use, I have not only, like Esau in some Degree been selling my Birth-Right for the deceitfull Morsal of this World's Meat, but like Judas, in some Degree been guilty of selling the Lord of Glory for the polluted Joy and perishing Treasures of this sinful World, and have murdered my own Soul crucified the Lord of Glory! O! what have I done, what have I done! And now my Sins have overtaken me, my Crimes have prevailed, and as Job saith of his Disease, my guilt and mine Iniquities bindeth me about as the Collar of my Coat; Vengeance hath pursued me, and all this is come upon me for my folly, and God is about to destroy me for my Sins!* But, Ah! little does the poor Soul know that God is now labouring for their good! they imagine that all their Happiness and Pleasures are now gone forever; they imagine that God is now angry with them, and is going to send them to Destruction: when it is quite the reverse; for God who feels a Pity for them is labouring to bring them to partake of Joys unspeakable to drink of the Rivers of Pleasure for ever more; Yea God is so far from desiring or seeking to be revenged upon them for their Sins, or sending them to Destruction, that he is now come to save them from Destruction, pluck them from their own Hell; and like Joseph, who understands their Language, tho' they cannot understand his he feels their Distress and condoles their Misery. Yea, and if I may use the Expression, his Bosom so burns with Love, and his Bowels so yearns over them with compassion, that he seeks a place to weep; that is, his pity and bowels of compassion that is undiscovered to the Sinner, is infinitely beyond what they could imagine, or what can be expressed to them Yea, as

132

little do Sinners know of Christ's pity for them as Joseph's Brethren did of his Compassion, when he was weeping in private, and they thought he was going to punish them, for no Sinner can see, feel or enjoy any Love in Christ, untill they feel him, theirs. And altho' the poor Sinner come trembling like a criminal to the Place of Execution, and thinks, that God is angry with them, and is going to destroy them: yet he has that Pity for them, that is unspeakable, and is now more willing to receive the returning Sinner than the Sinner is to return, and thus the Father sees the returning Prodigal, his Bowels yearn over him with compassion, and not only meets him, but runs to meet him, while yet a great way off.

O! be incouraged then to return ye mourning, Trembling Sinners starving for want of Bread, for God has sworn by himself, that he has no Pleasure in your Death, but that you turn and live.

Ah, saith the disconsolate Soul, *if I could see or believe that God had any Thoughts of Mercy for me, I should be incouraged, but I cannot see any Thing, but Blackness, Darkness and an angry God, and all Things seem to conspire for my immediate ruin.* Well, my Dear Hearers, did not all Things appear as desperate to Joseph's Brethren, but a few Moments before he made himself known to them, wiped all Tears from their Eyes, fed them from his own Table, and caused them to rejoice in his Favour?

Ah! And Jesus, who is present this very Moment seeking his Brethren, yearns over you with Bowels of Pity, is Ten Thousand Times more willing to receive you, feed you, and manifest his Love to you, than Joseph was to his Brethren. *Ah but* saith one, *I have Sold him, and crucified him, and how can be forgive me?* So had they sold their Brother, and been Guilty of the most inhuman Acts of Cruelty, and yet he could freely forgive them; surely you will not presume to say, or imagine, that he was more mercifull than the infinite Jehovah, whose Goodness, Love and Compassion is as boundless as himself: O then! Venture out against all those Discouragements, and cast yourselves on the Sinners Friend and he will deliver you! Ah, so free is his love, and so great his Pity toward you, that there is nothing keeps the Manifestations of his love from your Soul, this Moment, while I speak, but

133

your Bars of Unbelief! O, believe, believe, and all things are possible! Yea if ye had faith only, as a grain of Mustard Seed, that Mountain of Sin would be removed from your Soul, and your dead soul raised to life! O, that this migh[t] be the happy moment that you would now cast yourselves at the Feet of King Jesus, receive his Grace, enjoy his Love, and adore his name for ever, for he is now come to seek his Brethren. But to return to the Typical Narrative, O! how surprising, how joyfull, how affecting, and heartmelting was the Manifestation of Joseph to his Brethren! not a word or censuring or condemning them for their abuse to him: but with his Bowels yearning, and Heart melting, salutes them with a *come near I pray you, for I am your Brother, whom ye sold into Egypt, now therefore be ye not grieved, (k)* O! What love is now expressed in every Groan, Sob, Sigh and Tear, when their Hearts are too full to be expressed, and bursts forth in every Act of the Affecting Scene, like an overflowing Fountain, that has long been repulsed! But can no longer be contained; their breast thro their Bosom burn, and their Hearts dissolving in Love, unite as one, while their souls swoon (as it were) away with the Raptures of Joy at the happy meeting, and knowledge of each other. O! the affecting Scene! and think my Hearers, how great, how joyfull and unspeakable the Change! Yea, so great, and so obvious, that was I to assert that all this was imperceptable, and that Joseph's Brethren had no knowledge of their being forgiven, nor any Manifestations of Joseph's Love to them, I should be stared at as one almost bereaved of all Reason, repugnant to divine Revelation, and in the Face of the most glaring Demonstrations: And yet how many in this Land of Light will presume to declare, yea hold it as an Article in their Creed, that a soul may be converted and not know it! O, the Midnight Darkness of such Minds, and the Ignorance of such People, who pretend that so great, yea so unparrellel a Change can be wrought imperceptable to the Creature, on whom alone the Work is wrought! yea, so shocking is such a Principle, that was I to give you my Mind, it would be, that *it was contrived in Hell, and is vindicated* by none but the

(k) Gen. 45, 45.

134

Advocates for their dark Regions, for it strikes at the very Nature, design and consequences of the Kingdom of Christ among Men; for if there is no Knowledge, but only a guess-work, and all a Matter of uncertainty, who are the children of God, and who are the sons of Belial, or whether a man is converted or not, then the Pharisees, the Antinomians, Hypocrites, and the true Christians are all lumped together in one promiscuous Crowd, and there is no knowing how they will fare at the last, or which will fare the best: for a child of God, who is an Heir of Everlasting glory, does not know (according to that) after all his Pretensions of Religion, and love to God, and Knowledge of Christ, but he may be the next Moment lifting up his Eyes in Hell, and blaspheming the God that made him, and on the other Hand, the open profane who lives and dies without any knowledge of a Change, who are dying in the Gaul of Bitterness and Bonds of Iniquity, who have been making a Mock (as many do in these Days) of all pretensions to Conversion, or the Knowledge of the Gift of the holy Ghost, has as much cause to Die in Peace, and expect to be sliped into Heaven and made happy, as any of the Followers of the Lamb, which to me is so shocking and unreasonable, that if I could believe it I would this Moment close my Bible, and speak no more in that Name, nor ever more should you hear my stammering Tongue exhorting Souls to Repentance, and the service of God for if they were to seek, serve, and love and fear him ever so faithful, it would at last (according to that Hypothsies) be but an uncertain Matter.

O! why, why will Men love Darkness, choose their Bondage, and labour so hard against all true Reason, and divine Revelation, to reject the Truth, keep themselves in Blindness, and bind themselves down to perdition? who out of pretended Reverence, and (I was about to say bastard) Humility will reply! *Why god is a Sovereign, and therefore has a Sovereign Right to dispose of us as he please, without giving us any account whether he designs us for Happiness or Misery, and we ought not to be too anxious to know if he intends to save us or not, lest we are guilty of Presumption: but do the best we can, go trembling all our Days with a hope that he will not finaly cast us off, and if he does after we have cast ourselves on his Mercy, he will be just, and we shall have no cause to complain.*

And thus with all their pretended love, Reverence and humility they have brought forth a Brat, that if examined has been an Advocate for the Powers of Darkness, and a supported Antichrist for many Centuries, has made God a Liar, charged him with Cruelty and Injustice and sent many Thousands of Souls to Hell: For God has declared, that *he so loved the world that he gave his only begotten Son, that whosoever believeth in him should not perish, but have everlasting Life:* But some will say (who believe in an arbitrary partial God) *that is the elected Part of the world;* I wish they would let God speak for himself; who not only says for the world, but likewise goes on to tell the Reason, why, *that whosoever,* saith he, *believeth on him, should not perish, but have everlasting live,*[1] and then declares, that he would have all Men, to be saved and come unto the Knowledge of the Truth; *(m)* and then, lest we would not yet believe him, or should charge him with Neglect, Injustice, Cruelty and Partiallity, he swears as he lives (and commands his Servants in the same Verse to proclaim that oath) that he has no Pleasure in the Death of the Wicked (not the righteous, but the Wicked, he saith) but that (repeating over again, who he means) the wicked turn from his way, and live, and then goes on with a repeated call turn ye, turn ye, concluding with an expostulation, for saith he, why will ye die? *(n)* And now dare they say, after all he has declared, that we do not know whether he is willing to save us or not, or call it presumption to claim an assurance thro' his Word and Grace, untill we leave this Life, and with regard to knowing our particular Interest in this Truth, he declares in positive Terms, *ye shall know the Truth, and the Truth shall make you free; (o)* and declares that, he will manifest himself to his Children; *(p)* and pray, what is a manifestation, but making a Thing known? yea, even your common reason will teach you, that if things are not made known they are not made manifest.

Yea, what happiness, what Salvation, what Joy, what life, can it be, that a man can have and not know it? how can Christ be a Man's Friend, Companion, and Comforter, Joy

(l) Joh 3, 16. (m) 1 Tim. 2, 3. (n) Eze. 33, 11.
(o) Joh 32. (p) Joh 14, 21.

and Strength, and the Man not know that he has any Christ, Friend, Joy, Life, Strength, or Comforter? But saith John on this Point, *hereby know we, that we dwell in him, and he in us, because he hath given us of his Spirit. (q) And we know that we are of God (r) and he that believeth on the Son of God hath the witness in himself. (s)* And Job doth not say, I guess, but *I know that my Redeemer liveth;* and Paul doth not say, it may be when we leave this world, God will bring us to Heaven, but *we know that if this our Earthly House of this Tabernacle were dissolved we have a building of God an House not made* [*with*]⁴ *Hands eternal in the Heavens*, and David not only saith, that God hath made with him an everlasting Covenant, but offers to tell how he was brought to the Knowledge of it by his Conversion; *come* saith he, *all ye that fear God, and I will declare what he hath done for my Soul;* and saith the spouse, *my beloved is Mine, and I am his.* Yea, and so full is the Oracles of Life of this Truth, that if it was necessary, I might continue for an Hour, repeating such positive demonstrations from him, that cannot lye: and yet against it all, how many will labour to spread the Cause of Antichrist, and say *we cannot know, that we are converted in this Life*, and look upon it as I before observed, that they are doing God Honour, when they are saying, they must leave that with God, must walk Trembling all their Days, and not presume to intrude into the Secrets of God, to be so positive, whether or not he intends to save them. Altho' the true Christian's Saviour, saith to his Children, *let not your Hearts be troubled, for I will not leave you comfortless;* and saith the Apostle, when speaking in his Master's Name to his fellow Saints, *rejoice, and again I say rejoice;* And if you will but examine, you will find no sin that Christ ever reproved his disciples for so much as for Unbelief; even calls them Fools, and expostulates with them, why, and how long they would thus harden their Hearts by Unbelief? and yet now think they are doing God, and their own Souls service by nourishing and preaching up the Necessity of Unbelief? tho' they will not allow it is unbelief they are pleading for; because they will cover it with some more plausible Terms:

(q) 1 John 4, 13. (r) Joh 5, 19. (s) 1 Joh 5, 10.

but the Lord knows they have no cause to plead so much for the Necessity of slavish Fear, doubts and Unbelief, if it has been as cruel to their Souls as it was to mine; and as for those who argue, that people may be born again, and not know it, if I should be asked my mind to give the reason, why they argue so unreasonable and inconsistant, I should reply, *why from the cause, that a blind man thinks it strange, when you tell him that black is not white;* But has had too long; my attention has been stolen away from our subject to refute Inconsistences;[5] and therefore I return and O! what Joy, of soul, what melting of Heart, does attend the Manifestation of Jesus to his Brethren, or to the returning Prodigal! long has the poor Sinner been labouring hard to humble his Soul, and soften his hard Heart, to hate sin, love Holiness, to get some good Frames, and find some Evidences of Grace: but all was in vain: but now a discovery, and felt Sense of the Love and Compassion of Christ has done it in a Moment; for he looks on his Sins (and himself for his Sins and Folly) with Detestation; not because of its Condemnation so much as its appearing horribly evil in its Nature; and wonders that he could hug the Monster in his Bosom so long.

Now he sees that beauty and amiableness in God and his ways that his Soul falls in love therewith; not so much for a Shelter from Hell and misery, but for his life, his Joy, and his portion; not for the life to come only, or to be sure of some happy place after Death, but for his life, Joy and portion in this life, and wonders that he has not fallen in love with it long before.

And now, altho' he before like Joseph's Brethren expected immediate destruction and thought that there was an angry God coming out in vengeance against him, yet he finds that God is love, and has forgiven his sins with freedom; yea, he sees that he was so far from having any desire or design to destroy him that he has [not]p only forgiven him but would have forgiven him before if he had believed and cast himself upon him; and his very heart breaks as it were more for his rejecting and abusing such love than for destroying his own soul; and yet seeing yea feeling that God has so long been waiting, wooing and beseeching and now after all his innumerable offences has freely forgiven him, smiled upon

138

him, shed abroad his Love in his Soul, and loves him with an everlasting love and all this thro' the sufferings, bleeding wounds, and dying Groans of his best friend whom he has long dispised, rejected and Crucified by his Sins, and now while all this he sees, feels, knows and enjoys thro' the same meek and lowly Jesus that is now present with him and communing with his Soul, causes him, like our Type his soul as it were to swoon away with a rapture of inexpressible joy and his heart to dissolve with love that is stronger than death; and thus in love, joy, gratitude and humility, he swoons, if I may say on the Neck of his loving, forgiving, and long-suffering, Brother Joseph, while he on the Neck of the returned prodigal, their souls, if I may say, mingle and become one. O what love, what relenting, what gratitude, what humility do they feel, crying out within themselves, as the Patriarch at the news of his Son, it is enough, Joseph is yet alive! and O saith the soul he is my Friend, my Brother; Ah, he is my Saviour, my God, my King, my Father, my Husband, my Helper, my companion, my comforter, my life, my Light, my Leader, my Strength, my Joy, my portion and everlasting reward! but O these are joys that the stranger intermedleth not with; a white Stone and new name which no man knows but him that receiveth it; and therefore I cannot possibly describe them to you that are yet unconverted: But God knows I long to have you all participate in those unspeakable joys of the redeemers's love; yea, and it is with the greatest delight that I stand to speak to you in his Name to attract your minds to the glorious scene, and O that he might this night while I am speaking (like Joseph to his Brethren) manifest his love to your Souls! soon would you forget your sorrows, Triumph over your fears and foes, rejoice in God your Saviour, and say as the Queen of Sheba concerning the fame of Solomon, it was a True report that I heard of the Wisdom, love, beauty, goodness and glory of King Jesus, but the one half was never told me; O then be intreated to hear the calls of Jesus, who is come this night to seek his Brethren, nor will you ever enjoy a happy moment from this time forward forever until you are brought to a saving knowledge of this meek and lovely Jesus; O therefore he intreated my dear Hearers, to adhear to his calls, banishing the world with all its amusing charms and find place in your hearts for this waiting friend; this heavenly visitant, everlasting comforter, portion and reward. O, could I expell the interposing clouds between you and this Jesus, or unvail your dark minds but one moment, you would be so attracted with his beauties and so ravished with his Love, you would not only choose him for your present and everlasting all: but would be so attracted with his beauties and so ravished with his Love, you would not only choose him or your present and everlasting all: but would cry out against all other glories, beauties, Joys and delight, *O infamy, Misery, and Deformity!* But by reason of your blindness, darkness, ignorance and insensibility you are so miserably infatuated, as to pursue and expect happiness in the poor perishing amusements of this deceitful world, where happiness never was, or ever will be found, while in Jesus you see no form or comeliness of beauty that you should desire him; and yet flatter yourselves with the vain hope of going to heaven by and by, pray what heaven would you find, where you did not love the person who was all the glory and joy of heaven? or what happiness would it have administered to Joseph's Brethren at the time they were conspiring his Death with their breasts burning with rage, and envy to have been confined to his embraces with their heads on his breast? but when the love of Joseph had melted their hearts, slain their enmity, and expelled their prejudice, why then they accounted it both honours and joys unspeakable to fall in his embraces and enjoy his love.

And therefore never more let the devil make such fools of you as to expect ever to find or enjoy any heaven until you love Jesus for he will be a hell to you, and his love increase your torment far more than the wrath, malice and rage of Devils, unless your natures are changed and made like him; so that altho' the greatest part of Christendom vainly imagines, that it will be with the greatest reluctance to the wicked that they are forced or Driven out of Heaven, and imagine they would think it an unspeakable Privilege to be admited to be with God and his Angels; yet it will be so much to the contrary that they will think it the greatest Addition to their Torment to be so near to God, Angels and Saints as they are; and instead of praying for, or desiring to go to Heaven if they could, have their request answered, it would immediately be, to be at the most infinite

140

Distance from God, and all that was like him for God himself has declared that his Presence will be of such Torment to them, that they will call for Rocks and Mountains to hide them therefrom, and therefore never marvel any more at Christ's declaring, that ye must be born again; but make it your chief Concern to get out of your own Hell into the heavenly Jesus; and then you will find a Heaven wherever you may be, even if among Devils: But if you live and die in your Sins, you will forever be of that natural Enmity against God, that altho' your Miseries and Tortures are ever so unsupportable, yet you will be so far from any desire to be forgiven of God, helped by God, or happy in God, that you will with the greatest Rage abhor, dispise and reject him to all Eternity: O therefore! let me again drop a Word of Friendly Warning, and say as Lot to his sons-in-law, *up get ye out of this Place*, and cast yourselves on Jesus, who alone can change your Nature. But now I must return to a few more Remarks on our Subject. The Egyptians, observe, were neither in the Room, when Joseph made himself known to his Brethren, nor when they eat, did they eat at the same Table: for they thought it an Abomination to eat with the Hebrews. So let me tell you, that the Children of this World are not only (tho' bodily in the same Room) ignorant of the Manifestations of Christ to his Brethren; but likewise account it an Abomination to eat with them of the same Food.

But saith some of my Hearers, who never yet saw their own Hearts, the man is mistaken now, for God knows I would rejoice to set down with the Disciples of Christ to eat the same bread and Drink the same water. To which I reply, I doubt not, but some of you are sensible by the awakening Spirit of God of your miserable starved Condition, that you find the want of something; but do not yet want Christ, nor the bread of Life; tho' you may think, that you would come on any Terms, but the Truth is, you like the prodigal, when he began to be in Want, instead of going Home to his Father for bread, he rather chose First to go and join himself with a Citizen of that foreign Land, and therefore was not only as far from his Father's House as before, but likewise still starving and with the Swine, with nothing but Husks until he could live no longer there, and then he went home to his Father, and I would to God, that you who are in some degree awakened, and begin to be in Want of something, was likewise so starved out, that you could no longer stay with the Citizen of that Country, and then you would come Home and eat Bread with me in my Father's House.

But ah! the Language of your Souls are with all your good Frames, sincere Desires for to receive Christ, and be for him only like those who would take hold of one Man, and say we will eat our own Bread, and wear our own Apparel, only let us be called by thy name; (t) and so it [is] at last,[7] altho' you may think I judge you too hard, all is but your own bread that you want to eat: for that Moment you want Christ you will have him. But O I hope you will not be persuaded to come with all your Souls, without money and without Price, and receive Christ as he is, and you will soon set around my Masters Tables, and feast on the Wonders of redeeming Love, for the Lord is come, by a stammering Tongue to seek you. And altho' you find yourselves unworthy and unfit, with a hard Heart, a stubborn Will, and a stupid Mind, feeling yourselves barren without any Thing or good Frames to recommend you to God, yet come as you are, and you shall not go empty away. God will not reject you, because you are poor and miserable, without any thing to help or recommend you; and therefore, why O ye of little Faith, *why reason ye any longer, because ye have brought no Bread?* do not come to bring Bread or good Frames, but come and receive Bread, and thereby attain a soft Heart, and a humble Soul. Yea, and you may depend on it, that stay away as long as you will, to attain good Frames and Evidences of Grace, if ever you come to Christ you will come at last as dry and as barren as ever you felt yourself. O Try the Experiment this Night, cast your souls, and see if it doth not remove the Mountain of Sin, and melt the Heart with Love. But saith one would you have me presume to come just as I am now? No, my dear Reader, if you can ever get any better by staying away: but if not, I would have you come this Evening, and just as you are with all your Wants, sins and disorders. And let me ask you, if you wanted to melt a Body of Ice, would you move it to or from the fire? I dare say you will reply, why to

(t) Isa. 4, 1.

142

the Fire, For nothing else will melt it: so let me say if you want your hard Heart melted, your soul humbled, and your barren Mind made Fruitfull, fly with all thy Disorders to the warm Beams of that Sun of Righteousness, and the Mountains will flow down at his Presence, what would you have thought of the Serpent-Stung Hebrew, who for a cure had run from the brazen-Serpent, and instead of looking to it would look from it? look, O then, ye sin-stung Souls, look away to the glorious Anti-Type, and you will find an immediate and infallible Cure for all your Disorders; and this Night he is exhibited before you on the Pole of the everlasting Gospel. Believe, O ye Sons and Daughters of Adam, and live forever.

But our subject being so large, and breaking forth into my Mind with such Rapidity, that I am more at a Loss to know what to leave unsaid, than I be what to say; but lest by being tedious I should become unfruitfull I shall hasten to a few more Remarks, and conclude.

Joseph, observe, gave his Brethren change of Raiment, and so does Christ: for ever new-born Soul doth so far Partake of the Spirit and nature of God, that it not only cleanses them in a degree from sin and Vanity within, but likewise from without; it is the natural Consequences or fruits of that immortal Principle of Love, Christ formed in them the Hope of Glory to detest and forsake Sin and Vanity, and love and pursue Purity and Holiness; yea, and often Times they are so impatient for an immediate and complete sanctification, that they are crying out with Peter, *Lord not my Feet only, but my hands and my Head*, and blessed be God, the time is coming that will deliver them from all their Foes, extricate their weary Minds out of all their Disorders, and thereby bring a happy Period to all their sorrows: But O I could wish, that even the followers of the Lamb kept that divine Spark, immortal Principle, or Heaven-Born Mind so stirred up, and active, as would produce a more visible Change of Raiment to the World; for it is the Life, and Fire of Heaven within, that will make them shine without, and cause them to appear as Cities on Hills.

And as for you that never know the divine Love, I do not wonder, that it is so hard for you to break off from this Sin, and that Sin, and the other vain Practice, and to keep on an

143

external Appearance of Christianity, for it is all but dry Forms, and a hard Task without any divine Love, or heavenly Life to produce it.

O why, why will you try any longer to cover your Nakedness with FigLeaves, or seek the Living among the Dead? Ye are dead and nothing can do you good but that which gives you Life: O fly then to Christ! in him is Life, and he is come to give Life unto the World.

Get your Souls alive to God, burning with a Principle of Love to Jesus, and then it will be your Delight to run the Christian Race, forsake every Sin, and walk in the Ways of God. O hear the calls of Jesus! for in his Name I seek my Brethren. O that I might be the Means in the Hands of God of perswading one of this Society to throw down all their expectations of ever being any more prepared to come to Christ, and take hold of the Offered Saviour! Ah, I should think myself well rewarded for all my Labour! yea, and how would your own Souls rejoice in the glorious Liberty of the Sons of God? and will you not be persuaded? will not the Glooms of Death, nor joys of immortal life awake and engage your Hearts to say with Rebekah, *I will go?*

Come my dear Hearers, halt no longer between two Opinions, Life and Death has this Night been set before you, and if God, be God, serve him, or if Baal serve him. Nay, is it possible for you any longer to treat these Things as Matters of no Importance? Can you return to your former Sloth and Danger, and close your Eyes this night unconcerned? has the Lord sent me here only to amuse your minds and please your ears with a fine Story? Or do you think that all that God requires is just to comply with the Custom of attending with your Poor miserable Bodies, and when you return, say with Thousands *"Well, I think we have been entertained with a very good Discourse."* And if they can say so much as that, they think the[y] have done very well, and may go home and lay down in peace; I say will that suffice you to go upon with Ease?[8] If it is, the Lord have Mercy on you! for great, yea unspeakably great is your Danger. Well, but saith one, should I not judge if the Discourse be good? Yes, my dear Hearers, but let me tell you, that there is no Discourse can be good to you, but that, that tends to get you to Christ. And God did not send

144

me here to ask Sinners whether or not the gospel is True, or its Doctrines good: But to beseech them in the Name of the Lord to accept of the Gospel Proposals, and be reconciled unto God, that they may be eternally happy in the Enjoyment of that which now they are Strangers to. O then let me prevail with you my dear fellow Mortals to make the grand Enquiry, what blessing, what Knowledge of yourselves, and of Christ you have attained; and for your Soul sake do not go as stupid, and as far from Christ as you came.

Your everlasting Salvation is at stake, your life is as a bubble on the Water soon broke and gone; Time is ever on the Wing, and some of you on the Declines of Life, just drawing your mortal Days to a Period; and perhaps this Night gone for ever.

O what a lamentable Scene is your Capacity without a Christ! God knows my Heart condoles your standing and longs to be instrumental for your Good; and this night in the Name of Jesus I seek my Brethren. O, arise in the Name of the Lord, for ye are yet Prisoners of hope; and you that feel the least Movings of his Spirit, hear the glad Tidings spoken to you, *even to Day*, saith he that is now knocking at your Doors, *after so long a Time, if ye will hear my voice, and harden not your Hearts, ye shall find rest to your Souls.* O that I could incourage you to open the door that he might come in and sup with you, and you with him! Yea this is my Errand in the Name of him that bled and died for the World, to declare his boundless Love and free Grace to Sinners; and to invite [you] even from the broad ways, and Hedges, and Ditches, to the Marriage Supper of the Lamb.[9]

O come in, come in, ye Poor, ye blind, ye Sick, ye sore, ye Lame and miserable; for all Things are ready, and the God of the Armies of Israel has sent out for you and waits to receive you; Ah venter [venture] upon his Grace and all the Joys of Heaven are yours forever.[10]

Stand amazed O my Soul, while I feel and contemplate the importance of what I deliver! what immortal Crowns, eternal life cry'd thro' the streets among condemn'd and perishing Rebels as a useless Drug! Yea, and Jehovah himself the travelling Messenger; or shall I say the Sinner's Servants? labouring for the eternal Salvation; good Lord, and must I say the greatest Part of the World labours in Vain!

O! is it possible for Sinners to be so cruel to their own Souls! or can there by any here this Night, that can neglect so great Salvation? Will any of you, turn your backs on the Lord Jesus Christ, who is come in the Power of his Gospel to seek you? O hear, hear, ye Sons and Daughters of Adam for the Eternal God has stooped to labour for your Good, and is now calling you from the Depths of Misery, and Despair to immortal Glory; and will you not hear? Will you reject his Calls, abuse his love and sink your Souls in eternal Perdition?

Methinks I feel for your Souls, and can but again, and again intreat you not to suffer this evening to be eternally lost to your Souls. O think that your everlasting Salvation is now at Stake; and should you neglect a few more Hours, your dye is cast, your State fixed, and you gone for ever: But if you will hear the Voice of God, give up Soul and Body into his Hand, and receive his Love in your Hearts, be made one with the Lord Jesus Christ, and live in Glory for ever more; O conclude therefore,[11] my dear hearers, this Evening whether or not you will receive the glorious Offer, for the Lord Jesus is now come to seek his Brethren.

But lest I weary my Hearers I return to the last remark that I shall make on our Subject and conclude, and that is, Joseph sending for his Father, and settling of his Brethren in Goshen, that he might have them under his Care, to be as a Father to them, to feed them and supply all their Wants.

And O! let me tell you, as Joseph sent his Waggons to fetch his Father, and all that belong to his Brethren, so the Lord Jesus hath sent the Chariot of the Gospel to bring you down, you and your little Ones, and all that you have into Goshen, a Place of Rest and Peace, where you shall be under the Protection of the God of the Armies of Israel, and fed from the King's Table, even of the Banquet[12] of Heaven.

And now, O Sinners! O what can I say more? Will you leave your Bondage, your Misery, and your Famine, and go to a Land of Rest, of Peace, Liberty and Plenty? O that you would say as old Jacob said when the Message came for him, *"it is enough Joseph is yet alive, I will go and see him before I die."* And O let me tell you, that if you will go and see him, and eat of his living Bread, which he will freely give you, you shall

146

never die.[13] Come, my dear Hearers, methinks some of you will be persuaded to embrace the offer, and be eternally happy, for I am sure you have never found one Moment of peace or Happiness in all your Fatigues; no, nor you never will, for there is a Famine in the Land.

And being so happy as to find a Number of young People giving their Attention this Evening, who are now in the prime of Life, and who I dare say are seeking and expecting of Happiness in this World. I can but address them in a few Words singular, tho' I hope they have apply'd the whole that has been said already.[14] O let me tell you that I know by Experience, that all your Expectations will fail you; you may contrive your frolicks and balls, and rush into company and Revellings, but they will all deceive you and leave you at last a starving, and perishing Soul in guilt, Blackness, Death, and exposed to eternal Despair, For such Paths are Paths of Death, and such Steps takes hold on Hell. But O turn to my Jesus, my all, and my Master, who hath sent me this Night to seek and call you, and you shall find food for your Souls, Peace for your Conscience, Joy for your Hearts, and an everlasting Friend and Portion, when this vain world is no more.

O can you, can you reject such an Offer, and abuse such Love, and ruin yourselves for ever? Will you choose Hell before Heaven, Misery before Joy, Death before Life, and the Company of Devils before the Company of Angels? Good Lord is it possible? And can mankind be so infatuated? Bleed O my Heart, and burst my Eyes over the unhappy Beings.

But O let me hope, yea I can but hope, that there is some among this Society that begin to feel their Need of Redemption and groan for Help; yea I am convinced there is some. And O! let me intreat of you then, to exclude every amusing Charm, and give your whole Attention to the only Thing, for which you have your Being; and especially you my young Friends that are in the Bloom of Life, if you feel the least moving or call of the Spirit of God, O nourish it as the Welfare of [y]our precious and immortal Souls;[15] for if you stifle it, or crowed it out, it may harden your Hearts beyond all Recovery, and you mourn at the last, and say, *how have I hated Instruction, and my heart despised Reproof!*

I remember once discoursing with a poor Sinner on his

dying Bed who told me in some of his lamentable Discourse, *"Ah saith he the time was I had a call, and the Spirit of God striving with me; but now I fear the Day is over; for,* said he, *when I was about Fourteen Years of Age, I was awakened under the preaching of George Whitefield,* [15] *I felt the Power of the Spirit of God; and for a while I forsook my vain Company and Amusements, and gave my Attention to the Means of Grace: But O I turned away, and never experienced a saving Change! But from that time I grew more careless, and never had much Convictions or Concern for my Soul since, and now,* saith he, *I am Fifty Years old, and upon a dying Bed, without a Saviour; being a stranger to the New Birth.*

O take warning, take warning, my dear young Friends, and Now, while your Breasts are full of Milk, and your Bones are moistened with Marrow, make sure to flee from the Wrath to come, and marry the Lord Jesus Christ — marry the Lord Jesus Christ did I say? What may such Wretches as we be espoused to the glorious Prince of Peace! O yes, yes, it is a Truth declared by him that cannot lye; and this night O sinners, he is come to make you the Proposal: Nor does he seek his own Benefit as the Earthly Suitors, for they are Fond of seeking after Beauty and Fortune: But O let me tell you, that he will marry you without Beauty or Fortune; for you are not only Poor, miserable and starving; but are in Debt Ten Thousand Talents, and have nothing to pay, and by your Sins are deformed and as black as the lower Regions; and yet he will receive you in his Bosom, and make you his Bride for ever; for the offer is now made you, yea if I never see your faces more, and this should be the last time you should ever hear my Stammering Tongue, I must charge you to embrace the offer remembering where ever you are that such an Evening you heard the Lord declaring, by his Servant, *I SEEK MY BRETHREN.* My message is delivered.

A M E N.

NOTES:

1. In 1795 this *Sermon* was reprinted by "Blunt & March" in in Newburyport, Massachusetts under the title *A Gospel Call to Sinners*. The 1795 version does not differ in any significant manner from the 1783 *Sermon*. Where there is a difference, apart from a more consistent use of capitals and punctuation and spelling, the difference will be explicitly noted in a footnote. The *Fort-Midway Sermon* is used "Courtesy of the John Carter Brown Library at Brown University."

2. Again, the point must be made that it would certainly be interesting to know what these "small, but useful alterations" actually were.

3. This obviously was a "small . . . alteration."

4. See Alline, *A Gospel Call to Sinners*, p. 25, *"an house not made with hands. . ."*

5. See *ibid.*, p. 25, "But too long has my attention be stolen away from our subject to refute inconsistencies, . . ."

6. *Ibid.*, p. 26, "he has not only . . ."

7. *Ibid.*, p. 29, "and so it is at last, . . ."

8. *Ibid.*, p. 31, "I say will that suffice you to go and lay down with ease?"

9. *Ibid.*, p. 32, "and to invite you that are in the broad ways, and hedges, and ditches, to the marriage supper of the Lamb . . ."

10. *Ibid.*, "ah venture upon his grace, and all the joys of heaven are yours for ever."

11. *Ibid.*, p. 33, "and conclude therefore, . . ."

12. *Ibid.*, "banquet of Heaven."

13. *Ibid.*, "you shall never want."

14. This is an excellent example of how Alline would zero in on a specific group in his congregation.

15. Alline, *A Gospel Call to Sinners*, p. 34, "O nourish it as the welfare of your precious and immortal souls;"

16. This "poor sinner" was not the only Nova Scotian who would make a connection between Whitefield, who died in 1770, and Alline. In the revised version the "sinner" said "I had a time when . . ."

17. See some of the changes introduced in the final paragraph in the 1795 version of the sermon, Alline, *A Gospel Call to Sinners*, p. 35.

> O take warning, take warning, my dear young friends, and now, while your breasts are full of milk, and your bones are moistened with marrow, make sure to flee from the wrath to come, and marry the Lord Jesus Christ — marry the Lord Jesus Christ did I say? What may such wretches as we be espoused to the glorious Prince of Peace! O yes, yes, it is a truth declared by him that cannot lie; and this night, O sinners, he is come to make you the proposal: Nor does he seek his own benefit as the earthly suitors, for they are fond of seeking after beauty and fortune: But O let me tell you, that he will marry you without beauty or fortune; for you are not only miserable and starving, but are in debt ten thousand talents, and have nothing to pay, and by your sins are deformed and as black as the lower regions; yet he will receive you in his bosom, and make you his happy forever; for the offer is now made you — yea, if I never see your faces more, and this should be the last time you should ever hear my stammering tongue, I charge you to embrace the offer, remembering where you were, that such an evening you heard the Lord declaring, by his servant, I SEEK MY BRETHREN. My message is delivered.

A
BRIEF VIEW
OF THE
Religious TENETS and SENTIMENTS

Lately published and spread in the Province of Nova Scotia; which are contained in a Book, entitled "TWO MITES, on some of the most important and much disputed Points of Divinity, etc"

AND

"In a SERMON preached at Liverpool, November 19, 1782;"
AND, IN A PAMPHLET, ENTITLED
"The ANTI TRADITIONIST:"
ALL BEING PUBLICATIONS OF
MR. HENRY ALLINE

WITH

Some brief Reflections and Observations:
ALSO
A VIEW of the Ordination of the Author of these Books:

TOGETHER WITH

A DISCOURSE on external Order,
BY JONATHAN SCOTT
Pastor of a Church in YARMOUTH

Jude, vers 3. Beloved, when I gave all Diligence to write unto you of the common Salvation: It was needful for me to write unto you, and exhort you, that ye should earnestly contend for the Faith which was once delivered unto the Saints

Halifax
Printed by John Howe, in Barrington — Street
MDCCLXXXIV

151

SECTION XIII.[1]

This Section contains some Passages taken from a Sermon preached at Liverpool, by the same Author, with some brief Remarks on them. The Sermon on which the Remarks are made in this Section, has this Title prefixed to it, "A Sermon preached to and at the Request of a religious Society of young Men. united and engaged for the maintaining and enjoying religious Worship in *Liverpool*, on the 19th of November, 1782. By Henry Alline." The Text, Mark xvi. 5. *And entering into the Sepulchre, they saw a young Man sitting on the right Side, cloathed in a long white Garment: - - - - -*

I SHALL proceed in this Section as in the last foregoing, by inserting the Author's Words, and then making some short Remarks on them: And I would here inform the Reader, and the Public, that I have not this Sermon by me, for whence the following Qutoations [*sic*] are taken; I once saw it, and had the reading of it, and transcribed what here follows from it, with Exactness, for Ought I know: but in going over it the second Time, some Words may be missed or not placed right; and if it should so happen, I humbly hope it will be excused, as it will be what is beside my Intention, in that Case.[2]

I have no great desire to remark on the Heads of this Sermon; but as it may give some Satisfaction to judicious Readers, who always prefer the most plain and literal Meaning of the sacred Text (where it will bear and agree with other Texts) before any mystical and obscure Meaning not so plainly taught, and perhaps not taught in the Text at all; I shall therefore set them down; which are these, namely;

Page 6. "First. Follow the Son of God to the Sepulchre, and examine the Nature and spiritual Sense thereof.

"Secondly, The spiritual Meaning of this Young Man being in the Sepulchre.

"Thirdly. What we are to understand by this young Man being at the right Hand of Christ while in the Sepulchre.

"Fourthly, and lastly. What we are to learn of his being cloathed in a long white Garment and something of the Privileges of being thus with Christ in the Sepulchre."

152

Remark 1. These Heads of Discourse may serve to amuse some; and perhaps excite the Commendations of such as are lead by mere Sound rather than plain naked Truth, and the Simplicity of the Doctrine of the holy Scripture: but how they may serve to instruct the Ignorant, or edify a serious Mind that is in the Search after Truth, is not easy to determine. Besides, I do not remember one Word or Sentence dropped in all the Sermon, that discovered that this *Young Man*, as the Evangelist calls him, was truly and properly an holy *Angel* of God, sent from Heaven to declare the *Resurrection* of the *Lord Jesus:* I say, I do not remember a Sentence or Word in the Sermon that discovered this, tho' I will not possitively affirm it. Had he told his Hearers this, there would not, perhaps, have been any Thing in this Text, more than any other, that was adapted to the Occasion on which the Sermon was preached: And besides, when we consider the young Man in the Text to be an holy *Angel* (as he indeed was) three of his four Heads of Discourse are as impertinent and remote from the Text, and the whole Context, as any Thing; as it properly teaches nothing about a young Man, but an holy *Angel*. - - - - - - But I proceed,

Page 11. "And O! let me intreat my Hearers to shake off some of the Prejudices of their Education, and receive a Jewel that may not only be a Blessing to your own Souls, especially you who are in the Prime of Life, just coming out to espouse the Redeemer's Cause: but likewise arm you against the *Arian* and *Socinian* Invasions: For their Hands have been much strengthened against the Truths of the Gospel by many Preachers and Writers, who were labouring to vindicate the Gospel by holding forth that Christ, who was the very God, suffered and died to satisfy God; which the *Arians* and *Socinians* say, and well they may upon this Hypothesis, was God punishing himself to satisfy himself, and to fulfil some outward Law which Man had broken. And thus they say (using their own Comparison) he takes out of one Pocket and puts in the other; which indeed would be evidently inconsistent, as they observe. And yet it is held forth by every one who pretends that Jesus Christ died to satisfy something in God, which they call incensed Justice, and vindictive Wrath. O! my dear Hearers, banish, yea forever banish all such groundless, inconsistent, unscriptural, and God-dishonouring

153

Principles or Conceptions from your Mind."

Rem. 2. According to our Author, to maintain that Christ died to satisfy the *incensed Justice of God*, is a groudless, inconsistent, unscriptural, God-dishonouring Principle. But let our Author run on as he will, and charge the Principles of others with Things that they do not maintain, or hold any more than himself: Yet this we shall assert, That the *divine revenging Justice of God*, is a lovely, bright and glorious Perfection in the holy God; and it was altogether a becoming and glorious Act of Obedience for our Lord Jesus Christ to give his Life a Sacrifice to the *vindictive revenging Justice of God*, to atone for the Sin of Man! This has been attended to in Section fifth, to which the Reader is refer'd. Our Author brings in the Objection of the *Arians* and *Socinians* (as he says it is) to darken and reproach the Doctrine of Christ's Satisfaction; but he must make an open Retraction of what he has wrote, before the World, before we shall have any just Ground to think, that he does not deny the Satisfactioin of Christ, as fully and palpably as any *Socinian* has done since that Sect first rose up in the Christian Church. See this Author's Sentiments exposed, Sect. V. And what he has here asserted will shew that my Representation of his Sentiments there, was not contrary to what he has fully discovered here.

Page 12. "For if God hath made some such Law, the Breach of which will so incense him, that he must suffer to appease the Wrath and repair the Injury done to himself; then he hath not only made a Law to discover an austere and ostentatious Humour, but that exposes himself to an everlasting Loss and Injury. For, first, if Sin could break any such Law as would incense the Deity, then his Character is for every impeached; for the Wicked in Hell will be for ever perpetrating the same Crime, and consequently increase the same Injury to the Law, and Dishonour to his Name."

Rem. 3. Observe here, he saith, "If Sin could break any such Law as would incense the Deity, then his Character is for ever impeached." Here he calls in Question and denies that Sin could break any such law as would incense the holy God. According to this, Sin does not provoke or incense the just God, nor is he angry with Sinners, nor does his Wrath abide upon Sinners that are out of Christ, nor need they fear the

Displeasure of God overtaking them. And if God is not incensed and prvoked at the Sin of Man in breaking his Law, then Christ had no Need to substitute himself, and stand in the Room and Stead of the Sinner, and die for his Offence; for God was not, offended nor incensed against the Sin of Man according to our Author. And further, according to this, Devils and wicked Men have not offended nor incensed his Justice against them; they have not offended God, nor done any Hurt. Here is the Strain our Author has gone into to dispute away the Doctrine of Christ's Satisfaction to the offended incensed Justice of Goh [God] for the Sin of Man; which is the very Foundation of the Hope of a Sinner, and the only Door that is open'd to him for his Reconciliation to his offended God and dreadful Judge. True Faith in the Satisfaction that Christ has made to the incensed revenging Justice of God by his Blood, is the only sure quieting Consideration to the awakened convinced Conscience of the guilty Sinner. And how much our Author has done to pluck away this Ground of Hope, both here, and in his *Two Mites*, must be left to the Reader to Judge for himself. That God is offended, incensed and provoked with Sin, which is the Transgression of his Law, may be seen in Sect. V. where the Matter is stated and cleared, se [so] make Way to prove that Christ died to satisfy the incensed revenging Justice of God for the Sin of Man, to which the Reader is referred.

He goes on.

Page ib.[3] "Well; but saith one, which I know is the Reply of those who hold forth such an arbitrary incensed God, and rigorous, he will never punish the Wicked in Hell for the Breach of that Law. To which I answer, If I admit your Reply, yet you are still as deep in the Mire as ever: for you not only dress up a glorious Being in a ridiculous Habit, but likewise have fettered yourselves with as many Inconsistencies as ever. For you have thus not only declared that God is forever punishing the Wicked in Hell, to be revenged, or receive the Penalty as you say, of that Law which they have broken; but likewise that the Law must forever remain broken; for every Sin deserves, as I know you will say, everlasting Punishment. And as they are continually perpetrating their Crimes to an infinite Extreme; so that in Stead of God being even with them, the Penalty paid, or the Law fulfiled, the Breach is infinitely enlarged, the Injury increased; and therefore God and his Law for ever sustain an encreasing Loss; for they are forever encreasing their Rage and Rebellion against him. Besides, if God's Justice was incensed as you say, and his Wrath stirred up by so insignificant a Being (in Comparison of God) as an Angel or Man, who may not only stir up his Wrath, and incense him, but keep him so forever; then what sort of a God do you worship? For methinks you must be so well acquainted with the nature of any Being incensed, and stirred up in Wrath, as to know that a God incensed, or with Wrath stirred up in him, is not only a God incensed, or with Wrath stirred up in him, is not only a God injured and (*Page 13.*) wounded, but a God enraged: And a God thus injured, vexed and enraged, is a God in Passion, Misery and Torment; is a God in Hell. O how shocking are the natural Constructions of such a Principle. And yet I shall be branded as any Enemy to the Gospel, and set as a Mark for the Arrows of the Traditionists, because I oppose such Principles as hold forth the great Jehovah to be possessed of such a Nature as is the Nature of Devils."[4]

Rem. 4. Because some hold and maintain that Christ died to satisfy the incensed, revenging Justice of God, this Author says, "our Principles hold forth the great Jehovah to be possessed of such a Nature as is the Nature of Devils." Let the Reader see what Pains he has taken to fix this Charge upon us. But his Way of arguing does not in the least prove our Principle to be wrong, but only shews that he has no Way to vindicate his Cause, but by dreadful bald Assertions, and heavy Imputations against them that he means to oppose: Having no Arguments in his Favour, he thinks, that to blacken the Principles of others will serve his Turn. But he must know, that we look upon *divine revenging Justice* to be so far from being like the *Nature of Devils*, as he charges upon us, that we maintain, that it is a very lovely, bright, and glorious Perfection in the Supreme Being; and appears so in the Sight and Judgment of all holy Men on Earth, and in the Sight of the Inhabitants of Heaven. See this proved in Sect. V.

He goes on.

Page ib. "Well my dear Hearer, I have been obliged to make a long Digression, to discover and extract the Poison out of your

156

wretched Principle."

Rem. 5. All this Digression is made to discover and extract the Poison out of their wretched Principle. And did he make these poor young people at Liverpool believe that he got the Poison out of their Principle at last? If he did, I hope they will consider the Matter again. He goes on.

Page ib. "For blessed be his Name, he came down freely for my Redemption, and would have completed it, if the Hands of the Ungodly had never touched him."

Rem. 6. That Christ would have completed the Redemption of any one of Mankind if the Hands of the Ungodly had not touched him, is more than any one knows; especially, as it was the determinate Counsel of God from eternity that Christ should die by the Hands of Sinners, Acts ii. 23, and iv. 27, 28.

P. ib. "For as for the broken Law which he came to fulfil; true, it was broken indeed and he came to fulfil it But what was that Law but the natural Reflection of the divine Nature: And therefore when Man broke off from that God, or turned from the Tree of Life, the Law was broken in himself, (Page 14.) to his own Ruin. And now by Reason of the Contrariety of his Nature, the Reflections of the divine Nature (Law of the Tree of Life) became to him a flaming Sword."

Rem. 7. Here is the *Law of the Tree of Life*, our Author has brought in to help to support, and make out his strange and absurd Arguings. There is the *moral Law*, the sum of which is contained in the ten Commandments, Exod. XX. and the *ceremonial Law* which had *a Shadow of good Things to come, and not the very Image of the Things*, Heb. X. 1. and the *Law of Sin and Death*, Rom. viii. 2. and vii. 2. viz. the natural *Corruption* of the Heart, which is continually urging to Lust and actual Sin, and is a powerful Principle like a Law, to hinder and restrain even Saints themselves from that which is good and right, and is the greatest of all Impediments that they meet with to obstruct their Course in Holiness. Rom. vii. 23. And there is the *Law of the Spirit of Life*, Rom. viii. 2. viz. the Holy Spirit's Influence, regenerating and working the new and heavenly Life on the Soul, with great Power and Efficacy. And there is a fifth *Law*, of which God is the Author, called the *Law of Nature*, viz. a Consciousness of Guilt or Innocence in a

Man's own Breast, or the Knowledge of right and wrong. Rom. i. 32. and ii. 14, 25. But in all these, or in all the *Bible*, where is the *Law of the Tree of Life*, that our Author has brought in here? If he had Boldness enough to impose this upon the *Auditory* where this was preached: yet, is it not strange that he should thrust it out into the World? Could he think that he was in a World where every Individual was so ignorant and totally blind, as that not one of them would notice, or be able to shew the *Absurdity* of this *Novelty*, that is here introduced to support him in misrepresenting, reproaching, and villifying the Atonement and Satisfaction of the Lord Jesus, made to the incensed revenging Justice of God for the Sins of Men? And also in shamefully reproaching and abusing the soberest Part of the Christian World who profess and adhere to this precious Truth, as one of the principal Doctrines of the Bible?

He proceeds.

P. ib. "And therefore the whole Work of Christ is to heal the Wound, remove the Contrariety; and thereby fulfil the Law for, and in the Creature, and thereby bring him back again to an Union with, and Enjoyment of that Tree of Life in the Paradise of God."

Rem. 8. "The WHOLE Work of Christ is to heal the Wound, remove the Contrariety: and thereby fulfil the Law for and in the Creature," our Author tells us here. Rather than not wholly overthrow the Doctrine of Christ's Satisfaction to the revenging Justice of God for the Sins of Men, he will venture to tell the World in plain Terms, That "whole Work of Christ is to heal the Wound, remove the Contrariety, and thereby fulfil the Law for, and in the Creature." Now observe, If the whole Work of Christ was to heal the Creature's Wound, and remove the Contrariety within (as our Author expresses the Matter) or to represent the Matter more clearly, if the whole Work of Christ lay with Men, with Sinners, in regenerating and sanctifying them, and enabling them to fufil the Law, then the Mediation of Christ between God and Man is entirely overthrown at once. He is no longer a Mediator, if his whole Work lies with the Creature Man, in healing his Wound. If the whole Work of Christ lay with the Creature Man in regenerating and sanctifying him, not only is the Mediation of Christ between God and Man destroyed, but also

158

the Redemption of Christ by *Price* and *Purchase* is overthrown and destroyed entirely. Redemption by Christ is twofold, viz. (I.) By *Price* and *Purchase*. I Pet. i. 18, 19. *Forasmuch as ye know that ye were not redeemed with corruptible Things --- But with the precious Blood of Christ, as of a Lamb without Blemish and without Spot.* Acts XV. 28. *---feed the Church of God, which he hath purchased with his own Blood.* (2.) By *divine Power.* Psa. CX. 3. *Thy People shall be willing in the Day of thy Power.---* Eph. i. 19. *And what is the Exceeding Greatness of his Power to us-ward who believe, according to the Working of his mighty Power.* These are the Parts of Christ's Redemption which he performs in the discharge of the *Offices* with which he is invested as great and glorious Mediator between God and Man. In the Discharge of his prophetic and kingly Offices; he redeems from Darkness, Blindness, Obstinacy, Enmity and Thraldom under Satan, by instructing, renewing, sanctifying, protecting, and glorifying in Heaven at last: In the Discharge of his *priestly Office*, he gave his *Life* a *Sacrifice*, and shed his Blood to atone for the Breach of the Divine Law, and make full Satisfaction to the incensed Revenging Justice of God for the Breach of his Law, and thereby redeem Sinners from the Curse of it: And in the Exercise of his *Priesthood*, he ever lives making intercession for his People in Heaven. Now this Part of Christ's Redemption, namely, by *Price* and *Purchase*, which was the most difficult and Stupendous Work of our Redemption that Christ performed, our Author denies, and declares, "The whole Work of Christ is to heal the Wound, remove the Contrariety; and thereby fulfilled the Law for, and in the Creature." And all this is gone into, that he may support himself in opposing the Doctrine of Christ's Atonement to satisfy the revenging Justice of God for the Sin of Man.

Before ever this Sermon was printed or heard of, I was satisfied from what he had published in his *Two Mites*, &c. that this Author had overthrown both the Mediation and Satisfaction of Christ, if there was any Regard to be paid to his Words; as I have briefly shown in the fifth Section of this Treatise.

Our Author goes on,

P. ib. "And for this End he was obliged to enter into all the

159

Disorders and Miseries, yea I may say, Hell of fallen Nature, that is in this fallen and disordered Creature, to bear (and bring back from) all the Contrariety of their Hellish Natures; labouring by his own incarnate Spirit in the fallen Creature, until their Contrariety is subdued, and Will reclaimed and brought back from its State of Contrariety, to God again. And this Labour in the Hell of the Creature's Contrariety, was the Cause of his Suffering, when he saith his Soul was exceeding sorrowful, even unto Death: and this is the Way that God was in Christ reconciling the World unto himself; and declares himself that he suffered that Contradiction from the Nature of Sinners against himself, and even to the shedding of Blood, which Weight of Contrariety was the Cause of his Death. For when he entered in the fallen System at the first Instant of Man's Revolt, he became incarnate, for he was then in the Flesh, and that incarnate Spirit was labouring in and under all this Contrariety, (A Sepulchre indeed) until the Period of Time that he assumed a particular Body of Flesh and Blood, and then his Agonies of Soul which before was not visible began to appear: Yea, so great was his Agony of Soul or incarnate Spirit in the whole fallen System, that when there was no corporeal Punishment inflicted on his Body, or elemental Frame was crushed even to the shedding of Blood, under the infinite Weight of that contrariety which he was so related to.

"For you must not imagine that his Incarnation was only in that Particular (Pag. 15.) Body, but in all the Fallen System (centring to that Body) the Agonies of which forced the Blood through every Pore of his wasting Frame. And therefore it is very easy for you to see that the Jews were so far from being the Cause of his Death, although guilty of Murder in the strongest Terms, thet if they had never touched or laid Hands on his Body, he would, under that infinite Weight of that Hellish Contrariety, labouring in Agonies of Soul to carry on his grand Design, and reclaiming this fallen Nature, have soon expired and given up the Ghost; that is the Agonies of his Soul, for it was his Soul that, was made an Offering for Sin, being so much greater than his Body could bear, would so have crushed his Body as to overcome and put an End to his mortal Life."

Rem. 9. "And for this End he was obliged to enter into all the Disorders and Misery, yea I may say Hell of fallen

160

Nature, that is in this fallen and disordered Creature." This our Author says of Christ. What an idea of Christ is here conveyed? He entered *into* all the Disorders and Hell of fallen Nature, that is in this fallen and disordered Creature? The blessed *Jesus* partook of the *Infirmities* that accompanies human Nature since the Fall, such as *Hunger*, and *Weariness*, and *Pain:* But where are we taught in the History of his Life and Death on the Cross, that he entered into all the *Disorders;* yea, and Hell of fallen Nature, that is in this fallen and disordered Creature? The Second Person in the Adorable Trinity, in the fullness of Time, took the human Nature, consisting of a Body of Flesh and Blood, and a reasonable Soul, into a personal Union with his divine Nature: but this Nature that he assumed, was pure and holy, unspotted and unblemished, both in Soul and Body. He was a *Lamb without Spot and without Blemish.* I. Pet i. 19. A few Lines further, he says of Christ, "And this Labour in the Hell of the Creature's Contrariety was the Cause of his Suffering, when he saith his Soul was exceeding sorrowful, even unto Death." The holy Scriptures tell us concerning the Sufferings of Christ, Isa. liii. 5. 10. *But he was Wounded for our Transgressions, he was bruised for our Iniquities: the Chastisment of our Peace was upon him, and with his Stripes we are healed. Yet it pleased the Lord to bruise him, he hath put him to Grief: when thou shalt make his Soul an Offering for Sin.* The inspired Prophet tells us from whence Christ's Sufferings arose, when he says, *The Lord laid on him the Iniquities of us all, and bruised him, and put him to Grief, and made his Soul an Offering for Sin.*

But our Author tells us, that, "This Labour" of Christ "in the Hell of the Creature's Contrariety was the Cause of his Sufferings, when he saith his Soul was exceeding sorrowful even unto Death." Had our Author acknowledged the Truth, that the Soul and Body of Christ was made an Offering to the revenging Justice of God, under which he was bruised to make Satisfaction for the Iniquities which the Lord laid upon him, it would have overthrown his whole Scheme; and therefore he must invent something new, to account for the Sufferings of Christ, namely, "His Labour in the Hell of the Creature's Contrariety." This will do to amuse and confound the Reason and Judgment of those who will suffer themselves to be

161

imposed upon, by Words that are subversive of the Truth and Simplicity of the holy Scriptures; but never can tend to promote Godly Edification. He goes on to say concerning Christ, "For when he entered in the fallen System at the first Instant of Man's Revolt, he became incarnate, for he was then in the Flesh, and that incarnate Spirit was labouring in, and under all this Contrariety, until the Period of Time that he assumed a particular Body of Flesh and Blood; and then his Agony of Soul, which before was not visible, began to appear." Observe here, that Christ became incarnate at the first Instant of Man's Revolt; that is, at the Instant that our first *Parents, Adam* and *Eve* transgressed; viz. four thousand Years before his Incarnation that the Bible gives us an Account of. Further, the Agony of Christ's Soul was not visible till he took a Body of Flesh and Blood. Here he teaches us, that Christ had a human Soul before he had a Body; and he teaches that his Soul also was in the fallen Race; as may be seen in the very next Words to these last quoted, which are these, "Yea, so great was his Agony of Soul, or incarnate Spirit in the whole fallen System, that when there was no corporeal Punishment inflicted on his Body, or elemental Frame was crushed even to the shedding of Blood, under the infinite Weight of contrariety which he was so related to. For you must not imagine that his Incarnation was only in that particular Body, but in all the fallen System (centring to that Body) the Agonies of which forced the Blood through every Pore of his wasting Frame." Here our Author tells us, that the Christ he has in his Idea, was incarnate in all the fallen System and this before he took a particular Body (as he expresses it) and after he took a human Body too. Now the Reader must conjecture for himself what this Being can be that was incarnate in all the fallen Race even from the first Instant that Man fell. Whatever Being our Author intends, it is certain that the Lord Jesus Christ was never incarnate in all the fallen Race, (or System as he phrases it) nor yet was he ever *related* to the Contrariety of *Man's Nature*, as this Author here asserts. The human Nature which the holy Son of God assumed, was holy and without Sin, as the Angel declares to the Virgin Mary, Luke i. 35. ---*Therefore also that holy Things which shall be born of thee, shall be called the Son of God.* And although, by his assuming the human sinless Nature of Man, Christ is

162

become related to our nature more clearly than he is to the
Angels; yet notwithstanding this, he has not, nor ever had any
Relation to the *Corruption, Contrariety,* or *Defilement* of the
human Nature; but on the contrary, even with Respect to his
human Nature, he was and is entirely unconnected with it, and
separate from it. Heb. iv. 15. ---*But was in all Points tempted
like as we are, yet WITHOUT Sin.* Chap. vii. 26. *For such an
High-Priest became us, who is holy, harmless, undefiled,
seperate from Sinners, and made higher than the Heavens.*
That Text in I. Pet. ii. 24. *Who his own self bear our Sins in his
own Body on the Tree,* --- does not teach that Christ was
related to our Corruption, or was burdened or oppressed with,
or felt the least Degree of sinful Workings or corrupt
Inclinations, such as Men have, and such as the best and holiest
Men on Earth are burdened with, and groan under: But the
Truth taught here is, that Christ the Saviour of Sinners did
bear and suffer the Punishment of the Sins of Men, which Sins
were laid on him by Imputation, and the Punishment due for
Sin according to the Law was inflicted on him: and this agrees
with what was prophesied of him, Isa. liii. 6. *All we like Sheep
have gone astray: we have turned every one to his own Way,
and the Lord hath laid on him the Iniquity of us all,* Christ as a
Sin Offering did bear the Punishment of Men's Sins, both in
his Soul and Body; but never had any Relation to the
Corruption, Contrariety or Sin of our Nature, whatever our
Author may teach and endeavour to make People believe to
the Contrary.

I told the Reader in Section Vth, that the Christ which
our Author had in his View, and of which he had given the
World a Description, was something that was in each
Individual of the fallen Race of Mankind, and had been in
them ever since the fall of our first Parents; (though to tell us
what it is may be impossible) and I now leave it to the
Judgment of the impartial Reader, whether what is here
asserted in his own Words, does not give sufficient Ground for
such a Representation as I there gave.

But we proceed to take other Passages from our
Author.

Page 16. "I dwell chiefly on that which I trust you now
clearly understand; so that I hope you will never more imagine

that he punished himself (for he was God) to satisfy himself, or be at a Loss about his Death and Sufferings, for he suffered even the Miseries of Hell.

"And now if any of my Hearers should be at a Loss about God's Wrath, Vengeance, Anger, &c. (which the Scriptures so often speak of) let me inform them of two Things.

"First. That where there is Sin and Guilt, the Nature of God is to them as Wrath and Vengeance indeed; by Reason of the Contrariety which, as before observed, was the Cause of Christ's Sufferings and Agonies, when he had taken so much Sin, Guilt, and Contrariety upon himself; and therefore, wherever this Contrariety remains, the Nature of God will be as a Rock to grind them to Powder."

Rem. 10. Observe our Author here, he says, "where there is Sin and Guilt, the Nature of God is to them as Wrath and Vengeance indeed." Our Author had quite forgot what he had asserted a little before, it seems, in P. 12. where having observed that some hold that God "will forever punish the Wicked in Hell for the Breach of the Law;" to which he replies, "If I admit your Reply, yet you are still as deep in the Mire as ever; for you hereby not only dress up a glorious Being in a ridiculous Habit, but likewise have fettered yourselves with as many Inconsistencies as ever." According to our Author, to suppose or believe that God will punish the Wicked in Hell for ever, is dressing up a glorious Being in a *ridiculous Habit*, and fettering ourselves with Inconsistencies; yet he can here tell us, "That where there is Sin and Guilt, the Nature of God is to them as Wrath and Vengeance indeed." It may be he does not look upon this as dressing up a glorious Being in a ridiculous Habit, because he uttered these Words himself, and so may be inclined to think favourably of them. And as to its Inconsistency with what he has asserted before and after it in his Sermon, the Reader must be Judge for himself.

He proceeds to say.

P. ib. "Secondly. God in infinite Mercy condescends to speak to the fallen Creature as Things appear to them in their fallen State: But when you are wholly restored (Page 17.) back to God, you will find he will speak to you plainly without Parables; and likewise find that there is Nothing incensed in him; but you had been the wounded incensed and disordered

164

miserable Being yourself; and that it was in all these Disorders, Death and Misery that Christ suffered; and all to extricate you therefrom."

Rem. 11. Here our Author says, "God in infinite Mercy condescends to speak to the fallen Creature as Things appear to them in their fallen State." What an Insinuation is here, as though the true and holy God did not speak to us in his Word *as Things really are*, but only as they appear to us in our fallen State, and State of Blindness? How much does this look, as though the holy and blessed God kept back the Truth from Sinners, and when he tells them his *Wrath abides upon them*, John iii. 56. he only speaks to them as Things appear to them, but indeed are not as they appear to them? Here is a home Stroke struck to take off the Edge and Force of all the Threats of the divine Law that hold forth, in the plainest Manner, the unspeakably dreadful *Vengeance and Wrath* of God that is pointed against all unholy Christless Sinners, and which will lie upon them to all Eternity, if they die in their Sins. What easy Work will Sinners make of it, to get over all the divine Threats recorded in the holy Scriptures, upon this Principle? When the Sinner reads, *that the Wrath of God abides on all Unbelievers; and that cursed is every one that continueth not in all Things which are written in the Book of the Law to do them*, John iii. 36 Gal. iii. 10. he is furnished with Instruction from our Author, to still the Cries of Conscience, and quiet all Fears that may be raised and excited in the Mind, by referring to these Words, "God in his infinite Mercy condescends to speak to the fallen Creature as Things appear to them in their fallen State." And to this our Author adds, "But when you are wholly restored back to God, you will find he will speak to you plainly without Parables; and likewise find there is Nothing incensed in him." How directly do these Words tend to make the Sinner think that God has Nothing against him, nor is he angry with him, not incensed against his Sin; but only God speaks to him in his Word, as Things appear to him in his fallen state, but at the same Time, he is not angry nor incensed against him in the least? What an easy Matter will the Sinner make of it, to submit and resign himself up to God, in the belief of this Falshood, namely, That God is not angry nor incensed against him? It is an easy Thing for a Man to put is Life into the Hand

165

of his Friend, that he is sure has great Love for him: But it is a terrible Work to resign ourselves into the Hands of one, that we have greatly provoked and incensed by our Carriage towards him, especially when, he has Power and a just Right to take away our Life and Destroy us for ever; And this is the true state of the Case of Sinners; God is greatly provoked with them, and incensed against their Sin, and his *Wrath* abides on all Christless Sinners while they continue such. It is very easy for our Author to make Proselytes to his own Party, if he can make poor unthinking inconsiderate Souls believe that God is not angry with them, and that there is "Nothing incensed in him." When they are made to believe this Falshood, then can they love God, and be confident that he loves them; but the Bottom and Foundation of all is Deception. Sinners who indeed are brought to submit and resign up themselves to God, are convinced that God is greatly offended with them, and may very justly destroy them; and oftentimes they are under lively and awful Apprehensions that they shall be rejected, and that God will destroy them forever. The excellent Mr. *Stoddard* in his *Guide to Christ,*[5] when describing a false Submission to God which Persons deceive themselves with, he has these Words.* *"When Men submit to God as looking upon him as not very angry* Some Sinners submit to God, and at the same Time they think they have some Love to God, and some Care of his Glory; and accordingly they look upon their Peace half made; truly this is no difficult Matter; it is easy for a Man to put his Life into the Hands of his Friend: There is no great Opposition to submit to God, when a Man is pretty Confident that God *will save him*; but it is another Thing to submit to God, when a Man does not see a Spark of Goodness in himself, when he looks upon God as bitterly angry with him, and is much afraid that God will utterly destroy him: When Men submit under such Circumstances, it is evident that God has conquered them, and that their Wills are broken."

    It is an odd Business for any Person to pretend to undertake to preach the *Ministry of Reconciliation* to Sinners of Mankind (2. Cor. v, 18, 20.) and call upon them to be

* Page 94.

reconciled to God, which plainly supposes a *Breach of Friendship* subsisting between God and Man; and then to tell them, "there is Nothing incensed in God;" which in Effect is to tell them, that God has Nothing against them, is not angry, offended, or incensed against them.

I shall notice but one Passage more in this Sermon, which is this,

Page 26. "But I must now lead you to our fourth and last Observation, which was to discover the spiritual Meaning of this young Man being clothed in a long white Garment; and O that you may be seen to be thus cloathed all your days, and then may your Moments glide away with Joy.

"First. They are internally made Partakers of the Righteousness of Christ; not imputed as many imagine just to cover up their Sins, or any Thing done for them in some distant Region, to answer the Penalty of some outward Law, and thereby stand their Intercessor at a Distance; but the pure Spirit of Christ in them."

Rem. 12. Our Author under this Head of his Discourse, undertakes to discover the spiritual Meaning of this young Man being cloathed in a long white Garment: But why did he not tell his Hearers the *literal Meaning* of the Words in the Text, and discover to them, that the young Man cloathed in a long white Garment, was Nothing more nor less than an holy Angel of God, sent on a particular Message, viz. to declare that important and glorious Event of the Resurrection of Christ, the Lord of Angels, and made such an Appearance *(perhaps by assuming an airy body, as is thought by learned Men that the Angels often did when they appeared to, and conversed with Men)* as his Lord and Master saw fit that he should on such an Occasion? Had he told his Hearers this, he would have laid a Foundation for just Thoughts and Conceptions about the Sense of the Text, and any just and proper Inferences drawn from it. But not a Word of this Kind, that I remember, either here, or any where in the Sermon. He goes on to say, that the spiritual Meaning of this young Man being cloathed in a long white Garment is, "First. They are internally made Partakers of the Righteousness of Christ, not imputed as many imagine, just to cover up their Sins, or any Thing done for them in some distant Region, to answer the Penalty of some outward Law, and thereby stand their Intercessor at a Distance; but the pure

Spirit of Christ in them." What Treatment does the holy *Law of God*, and the *imputed Righteousness of Christ* meet with from our Author here? I do not suppose but that many Persons abuse the Doctrine of Christ's Righteousness imputed, by making it a Pillow for their Sloth and Disobedience, and if the support of their false Confidence and Hopes; but this gives no just Ground to think any more lightly of this important Doctrine, much less to reproach it, and treat it as not worthy of our Regard. Our Author when he is speaking of the Righteousness of Christ, says, "Not imputed as many imagine, just to cover up their Sins." The Imputation of Righteousness to cover our Sins, is derived, and treated with Disapprobation by our Author, but it is treated with great Veneration both by *King David* and the *Apostle Paul.* Psal. xxxii. 1, 2. *Blessed is he whose Transgression is forgiven, whose Sin is covered. Blessed is the Man unto whom the Lord imputeth not Iniquity, and in whose Spirit there is no Guile.* Rom. iv. 5, 6, 7, 8. *But to him that worketh not, but believeth on him that justifieth the Ungodly, his Faith is counted for Righteousness. Even as David also describeth the Blessedness of the Man unto whom God imputeth Righteousness without Works, saying, Blessed are they whose Iniquities are forgiven, and whose Sins are covered. Blessed is the Man unto whom the Lord will not impute Sin.* I. Cor. i. 30. *But of him are ye in Christ Jesus, who of God is made unto us Wisdom, and Righteousness, and Sanctification, and Redemption.* Phil. iii. 9. *And he found in him, not having mine own Righteousness, which is of the Law, but that which is through the Faith of Christ, the Righteousness which is of God by Faith.* Here are a few Scriptures which hold forth the Imputation of the Righteousness of Christ to Sinners of Mankind that believe in him, so plainly and fully, that our Author must not think that we shall all quit our Belief of this precious Doctrine because he has discovered a Dislike of it. The holy Scriptures hold forth two Way of Justification; the one by a Man's own *Righteousness* or Works of Obedience and Conformity to the holy Law of God, Rom. iv. 2, 4. the other Way of Justification before God, is by the *Righteousness of Christ* imputed to a Sinner and received by Faith alone. And this latter is the only Way in which Sinners of Mankind are to seek and expect Justification and Acceptance with God, because all are

168

involved in Sin and none keep the Law, and therefore none can be justified by their own Righteousness. Rom. iii. 22, 23, 24. *Even the Righteousness of God which is by Faith of Jesus Christ unto all, and upon all them that believe; for there is no Difference: For all have sinned, and come short of the Glory of God; being justified freely by his Grace, through the Redemption that is in Christ Jesus.* Deny the Imputation of the Righteousness of Christ, and you shut the Door of Justification and Acceptance with God against Sinners, as to the procuring Cause of it. By the Imputation of the Righteousness of Christ, I understand the reckoning or accounting his Obedience which he performed to the Law of God thro' the whole of his Life to the Death, to Sinners that believe in him, so as that they shall receive the Benefit of his Obedience as much as if they had performed it in their own Persons. Our Lord Jesus Christ fulfilled the Law perfectly, and *was obedient unto the Death, even the Death of the Cross*, Phil. ii. 8. and those who receive him, and are united to him by divine Faith, are Partakers of the Benefit of his glorious Obedience; hence he is said to be made of God unto them *Righteousness*, as well as Sanctification and Redemption, I. Cor. i. 30. And Believers place their Hope and Dependence on this Righteousness of Christ, and desire to be found in it and make their Appearance in it before God at last. Phil. iii. 9.

Our Author allows of no Imputation of the Righteousness of Christ to Sinners, "but the pure Spirit of Christ in them;" in which Expressions he confounds, or rather wholly excludes Justification by Faith in the Righteousness of Christ, while he is teaching the Infusion of Grace into the Soul in Regeneration and Sanctification. But we must not give up the Doctrine of Justification by the Righteousness of Christ imputed, to make Way for the Doctrine of Regeneration and Sanctification by the holy Spirit, seeing both are taught with great Plainess, and the former as well as the latter in the holy Scriptures; and have a perfect Consistence and Agreement with each other: And as Things are constituted, the former is as absolutely necessary and essential to our Salvation, as the latter.

Here are a few Passages taken from this Sermon, which, together with the Remarks that are briefly made upon them, will help the Reader to see what an Agreement it has with his

Book that we have made some Remarks upon; and also help us to form some Idea in what Manner the *Auditory* was entertained where this Sermon was preached. The second Time our Author came to *Yarmouth*, was upon his Return from *Liverpool*, in February the 6, 1782. and he tarried till the 19th Instant, thirteen Days inclusive of the Day he came and that on which he went away;[6] in which Time, according to the Informations I had, he preached eighteen or nineteen Times. Now we cannot suppose that there was much Study joined with his preaching; and we see here something of what is in one of his most correct Discourses, as we may conclude it to be, as he no Doubt reviewed it after the preaching of it before it went to the Press: Now what may we reasonably suppose there was delivered in eighteen or nineteen Discourses delivered in so short a Space of Time, by a Person that made little or no Use of Study or Notes, as may be supposed was the Case with our author, though I did not see him in this Space of Time?[7]

NOTES:

1. Pp. 169-189.

2. The Scott transcription of the Alline sermon is remarkably accurate. He may not include a word here or there and he may change the spelling of certain words, as well as revise Alline's unique punctuation and capitalization policy. But Scott never distorts what Alline actually wrote.

3. *Ibid.* The reference is to page 12 of the November 19, 1782 *Sermon.*

4. Scott concentrated his criticism of the *Sermon* to its five or six pages concerned with the Atonement. He obviously felt that Alline was especially vulnerable in this key area of his New Light theology.

5. The Reverend Solomon Stoddard (1643-1729) wrote *A Guide to Christ or, The Way of Directing Souls that are Under the Work of Conversion* (Boston, 1714).

6. For Alline's description of his February, 1782 Yarmouth-Chebogue sojourn, see Beverley and Moody, *The Journal of Henry Alline*, p. 191.

7. After reading Alline's three sermons and Scott's critique the reader may still wonder why these three sermons — and only these three sermons — were ever published. There are, I think, at least three possible reasons. First, by late 1782 and early 1783 there was a growing realization among his followers that Alline was close to death and they therefore wanted some visible and printed sign of his powerful spiritual message. Second, it should be realized that the Liverpool region was the most prosperous Yankee area of Nova Scotia and financial support for the publication of the sermons was readily available. Third, the evidence suggests that Alline had his greatest impact on Nova Scotia in the Liverpool region and this may help to explain why his followers there were determined to have these three sermons published as soon as possible. They would not only honour Alline but also their own

spirituality.

Despite the fact that the three sermons highlight Alline's unorthodox and highly personal preaching style, they were preached without the wild and extravagant gestures of his New Light followers. Simeon Perkins never criticized Alline's preaching style regarding it as part of the New England Evangelical heritage. Perkins, however, denounced the "Wild & Extravagent Gesturing" and the "over Straining his Voice" of Allinite preachers such as Harris Harding and the young Joseph Dimock. (Harvey and Fergusson, *The Diary of Simeon Perkins 1780-1789,* pp. 354-5.) Alline did not preach with a high-pitched "Yankee New Light whine" but rather made excellent use of his melodious tenor voice.

INDEX